CONFESSIONS OF A
TRANSSEXUAL PHYSICIAN

JESSICA ANGELINA BIRCH

ISBN-10: 1468158694
EAN-13: 9781468158694

In sharing herself with others, Jessica Birch writes a thoughtful analysis of her personal journey transcending the boundaries of sex and gender. Insightful and witty, her perspective on being a transsexual is both heartfelt and at times humorous. She presents a realistic view of what a gender transition can mean, both to the individual going through the process as well as to family, friends, and loved ones. She also celebrates the power of claiming her gender identity without losing sight of the adversity that surrounds her. With great determination and courage, she struggles to build a meaningful life. Having attained a new sense of self-worth, she now reaches out to help others who may also experience themselves as being transgendered.

—Christine Becker LICSW

CREDITS

I would like to give special thanks to the following people
who helped me write this book:

Nita Van Zandt and Eva Blue for editing
Evoryan Zafir for his illustrations
Clint Sloper for photography
Special thanks to all my family, friends, and patients for
their support over the years.

PREFACE

This book is a compilation of many short stories I have written and saved over the past seven years. Initially, I didn't think that I would make them into a book. I simply wrote them to capture what I was feeling at the time, because the emotional impact of each event relating to my transition was so strong. At some point though, it became important for me to give them a greater meaning and to link them all together. They became, in a way, a catharsis. I needed spiritual healing, and as much as I looked to others hoping that they could help me, the real healing had to come from within. Finding it has been painful at times, and I can't say that the process is over yet, but at least the shame and the feeling of deceit that I felt during the first forty-eight years of my life is no longer present.

Writing, like other forms of art, has given me a means to express myself. What ever good or bad that can be gained from it, however people perceive me, I can only say that I've felt it necessary to write down my thoughts for other people to read so as to give testimony to my life.

The greatest flaws in my personality are that I fear being alone, and I can be quick to find imperfection in others when I know that perfection doesn't exist in myself. Sometimes, in trying to be totally honest about how I felt at a particular time, I may come across as being a little self-centered. I realize that is one of my shortcomings, and I want to reassure the reader that it has never been my aim to portray anyone in an unfavorable light, and if my writing suggests that, I apologize.

My strengths are that I strive to find ways to see the good in humankind and I'm a strong believer in the power of forgiveness. I feel best when I'm helping others. It gives me a sense of purpose.

I hope that those who read my story will find my intentions genuine. All I want is for the world to pardon my actions, to forgive me for wanting a different life. I crave to be loved, desperately at times, but generally find it to be just outside my reach. The fact is, I often feel insecure.

As a physician, I have often found myself in emergency situations where I've had to make decisions quickly, decisions that might affect whether a person lives or dies. When this happens, I first say to myself, "Don't panic," and then something comes over me; it's like a higher being works through me. With a commanding presence, I hear myself shouting out orders to others like the captain of a ship, but when it's all over and I can be myself again, in quiet solitude, all I can think of is that nine-year-old boy who I once was standing out in right field just praying that I'd catch the ball if someone hit it to me.

Life is a game; it's part strategy, part fortitude, and part dumb luck if you're able to win. We try to understand how others perceive us by examining our reflection in the people around us, but we never know for sure if we're projecting a true image of ourselves. For whatever reason, we find the confirmation important.

As I wrote the various stories for this book, I told myself not to hold anything back, to be as true to myself and others as I possibly could, even if it meant exposing my weaknesses or allowing my thoughts to run naked without putting up a front. I put it all out there, so to speak, recognizing the potential consequences, because I want people to see how the mind of a transgendered person works—my mind—the split I always feel in my psyche, and I hope that people will find a way to empathize with the craziness that goes on in my head and realize that transgendered people don't choose to be the way they are but rather it's inherent within them.

I want to make the world better for future generations of transgendered individuals. It's my hope that those who read this book will find compassion for me and for those like me. What I felt, how I perceived events, my justification for my actions, and all the emotions I experienced while writing this book were real to me at the time. Through my character, I hope to provide people with a portal through which they can view the motivations of a transsexual person and thus better understand gender dysphoria.

I believe my life changed dramatically once I was able to embrace my transsexuality. Now that my transition is complete, I can see the events of the past in a broader perspective. My sexuality is just one aspect of who I am. I'm glad I found a way to be the person I always wanted to be, but it's not the most important thing in my life anymore. Granted, it was for a period of time. In fact, it was such an epic part of my life that I felt the need to write this book and leave a legacy to those pondering a path similar to the one I chose.

I crave normalcy now. I want to leave the past behind and build a life again with someone new. I hope that's possible.

After changing my sex, I chose not to relocate. People sometimes ask me, "Why didn't you move to another city or state after your transition, a place where no one would know you, so you could start over? Why write such a book as this? Why risk the possibility of disapproval and condemnation?"

The answer is: no reproach could be as bad as a life without fulfillment. I'm aware of my vulnerabilities, but there is a destiny I need to fulfill. Hiding from my past and trying to live in the shadows is not a good solution for me. I don't feel I have that much time left, and I'm willing to own up to the person I am if it helps me find God's grace. That's what it's all about for me. May the powers of the universe judge me favorably some day.

TABLE OF CONTENTS

Suicide	1
Early Years	5
The Birth of Two Selves	13
Crisis	25
Finding a Confidant I Could Trust	31
Time to Tell	34
Beginning the Transition	39
Meeting My Therapist	42
The Process Begins	46
Sex, Gender, and Metamorphosis	50
Informing One of My Closest Friends	54
Another Friend Learns My Truth	58
Family	61
Finding Out More	67
My Day at Bloomingdale's Department Store	72
Tulips and Dandelions	76
Moving Forward	82
Trying to Find My Way	88
Did I Kill Jake?	95
Hoping to Keep My Job	101
Changing My Voice and More	105
Prejudice and Advocacy	109

Thoughts, Truth, and Honesty   113

Surgery in Montreal   117

Moving On   131

Realizing I Had Support   135

Coming Into My Own   139

Feeling Estranged   143

Making It On My Own   152

The Choice   157

Grieving My Loss   164

Dancing, and Remembering   167

Reuniting With My Brother   173

Reconciling With My Mother   178

Conquering My Inhibitions   182

The Final Truth   187

Afterword   192

SUICIDE

For many years, I wished I were born a girl. I can remember, as early as four or five years of age, standing on my bed in the partial darkness of night, wrapping a blanket around myself playfully to make a dress. In an adjoining room, my parents' voices were a distant drone. I was at peace with the world, oblivious to male and female reproduction or how the human species perpetuates itself.

Tonight I was riding my bike, and I kept going around in circles. I was thinking of ways to stop the torment. Thoughts of coming out to Dr. Gransby recently, about my gender dysphoria, were fresh in my mind. Gender identity is a sense of self, a concept that relates to your sexual being, not something learned but rather inherent within you. I believe this, and I think I was born with two selves: one male and one female. Is that possible? Can there be more than one area of central intelligence within the brain? It's hard to explain to others how I feel sometimes. How can the majority of human beings understand something that's foreign to them if they've never had the experience? If it's not true for them, then they must either act on faith, believing what I sense about myself is correct, or take the alternative course and say I'm crazy. I'm tired sometimes, tired of living in a world that can't understand Jessie and me, a world that can't see Jessie like I do. I feel her emotions and join in her femininity. We have a love for each other because we are two, and yet we are one.

I began thinking of ways to end my life. I thought of buying a gun. I could imagine the weight of it and the coldness of the steel. I imagined placing one bullet in the chamber and giving it a spin for luck. I then came across a stone bridge with a ten-foot drop to the rocks and brook below. I thought of getting up a lot of speed on my bike and riding off of it, but it seemed too painful. I kept riding over the same trails again and again. Then I saw a clearing. It was far from the usual bikers and hikers and somewhat concealed. What if I waited for a nice sunny day, cut my wrists, and took a sedative like Bosomin. That might work.

I went to bed around ten thirty that night, and I couldn't help thinking of what I had thought of earlier in the day. I started dreaming, and I imagined a forest with an open field and some rolling hills. The clearing was totally concealed from the outside world. I could smell the grass and the trees, and it was beautiful. It was just before dusk and a little cool but still warm enough that you didn't need a jacket. I laid a blanket on the ground, and I looked off to the right at the sun and the moon. There were small clouds moving slowly in a circular fashion, and the leaves rustled gently.

As I laid there, Jessie and me, peace and tranquility abounded. I was wearing my Ellen Tracy prescription eyeglasses and a little lip gloss. A ceramic flower earring was in my left ear, and I had my butterfly necklace on. I was wearing a bra and a pretty lavender camisole. I loved the feeling of the straps on my back. I had shaved my body clean of unwanted hair, painted my nails, and wore my favorite ankle bracelet and toe ring. On my right thumb, I had a beautiful handmade ring with a pink stone, and on my wrist, a Fossil watch with a pink band and a butterfly face that blinked.

I turned my cell phone on and proceeded to take the Bosomin. Then I called Dr. Gransby's office and asked to speak with her. We had only known each other for a few months now, but I felt a connection to her; she was as much my friend as my personal physician. She asked me where I was, and I told her I was in a happy place. She wanted more information, and I told her I was in the forest. Sensing she was perplexed, I asked her why she couldn't hear my cries for help, and there was silence. She asked me if I was planning to hurt myself, and I hesitated. I had never asked anyone in my life for help before, and I couldn't understand why the world rejected me. Was I that ugly? I pulled the box cutter blade from my pocket and held it to my left wrist. I could feel a tear on my cheek. I didn't want to do this.

"Jake, where are you?"

"I'm in the forest" I replied.

"Let me help you."

I was starting to feel a little sleepy, and I could hear some birds chirping. I proceeded to tell her about Jessie. I told her I needed help and that I didn't know who I was anymore. I told her how I wished I had been born differently. I told her how I liked watching *Sabrina, the Teenage Witch* and old Hilary Duff shows on TV. I told her about the My Scene Barbie dolls that I take out of hiding when Marge and the kids go away for the weekend; there was Madeline, Chelsea, and Noel, to name a few. I held the blade a little closer to my wrist, and I gently made the first cut.

Dr. Gransby pleaded, "How can I keep you from hurting yourself?"

I answered, "You can talk to me, as a friend. Tell me what it's like to be a girl. Let me talk to you at the end of a workday, without a time limit, sitting next to you. We could sit at your office, a coffee shop, or a park. I won't touch you or hurt you. I just want to sit close to you and talk. I could bring black raspberry ice cream." There was again silence for what seemed an eternity. I pressed the blade a little deeper.

"Jake, if I agree to do this, will you see a counselor?"

I started to cry and I looked at the sky and I could smell the trees again. I thought how silly I must look laying here dressed this way. How did all this happen to me? Could I ever be normal? I had read about people like me in medical school. The textbooks stated that the cure rate was dismal and the condition not well understood. I took some of the pressure off the blade and dropped it next to me. I lay there with my hands at my sides.

"So peaceful here," I thought. I had only taken a single dose of Bosomin, just enough to help me fall asleep.

As I drifted off, I could hear Dr. Gransby's voice in the distance. "Jake, are you still there? Don't fall asleep; we want to help you."

I'm not sure when this story began. I'm not sure how it ends. Who are we? What makes us who we are? Maybe I should have let the blade go deeper.

EARLY YEARS

I was born Jacob Everett Mathewson in 1957, the year Elvis Presley first
appeared on *The Ed Sullivan Show*. Dwight Eisenhower was beginning
his second term as president, and the American Civil Rights movement
was just beginning. It was the post-World War II era—a time when only
a man wore a hard hat and only women were allowed to bake apple pies, a
time when children still etched their initials into wooden desks at school
and every soldier was a hero.

My first memories of childhood have become vague snapshots of a time
long past, with colors muted and images lacking distinction. When I was
two or three years old, I remember my mom talking to my dad about
a skunk in the backyard of our apartment complex and how it wouldn't
budge from a window well. The event captivated my attention because as
I watched from the living room, my parents in the kitchen, distant, and
occasionally glancing toward me, I somehow knew that the three of us
were connected. It's strange how events like this stick in your mind. We
lived in veterans' housing, built sometime after World War II, consisting
of long rectangular buildings with drab, reddish-brown shingles, carports,
and kids' bicycles lying on uneven front lawns. Dented metal trashcans

sat next to side doors, and patches of bare earth were visible between the hastily mowed grasses. I remember watching *Captain Kangaroo* on a black-and-white TV in a room with very little furniture, the walls and carpeting permeated by the color green.

There was a playground down the street from our house where kids gathered in a sand lot that contained a large metal swing set. Once, when I had gone there to play, a girl somewhat older than me stuck a lollipop in my hair and stole my tricycle. As if viewing the event from a director's chair, I have a memory of standing motionless, crying, and bewildered, as I experienced cruelty for the first time in my life. I suspect we all have a memory of something like this happening to us in our past. The world is not always a safe place, and fairness is an ideal that nature doesn't generally acknowledge.

When I was three years old, we moved to a third-floor apartment in Montague, Massachusetts. The stairs to the apartment always seemed steep and narrow. My parents' bedroom was actually an unfinished extension off the front of the house. We had a white cat named Fluffy, and my dad would bring home turtles from the Five and Dime store that we'd keep as pets in a small dish that included a plastic palm tree. I remember walking with him to the penny candy store to buy gumballs and watching him, without much success, try to grow a vegetable garden in our back yard. I remember lying on a hammock on a hot summer day, eating freshly baked chocolate chip cookies. And I recall a wasp stinging me while I played in a sandbox with a couple of older boys who told me, "If you don't bother it, it won't bother you."

I remember my mother apologizing to her friends about me while I sat on the toilet one day, as if I had some sort of illness or rare disease. That memory would only make sense to me in later years when I would learn that I was born with a genital birth defect.

When I was five years old, we left Montague for a new home in Greenfield, Massachusetts. On the day of the move, I remember it being a summer day with the sun shining and my dad smiling while he stood next to an old truck he borrowed packed with our belongings. It had tall wooden side rails, and the metal was dull and darkly painted. A mattress stood on its side against one of the rails, and it acted as padding for the furniture tied down next to it. I can't recall much else from that day and have little further recollection of the move. I was likely too small to be of much help and too young to truly appreciate the excitement of the moment.

Our new home had three bedrooms and was set on a postage stamp lot that cost all of about $8000 in 1962. My best friend was Tim Beaton, who lived just around the corner. I don't think his parents really planned him, as they already had two children who were grown and had since moved away. For that matter, I don't think I was planned either. My parents were married in November, and I was born in May. The math just doesn't add up, but that's another story.

Shortly after moving into our new house, my dad had an industrial accident. He was working at the local tap and die when he got his right hand caught in a lathe machine. He lost half of his index finger and required surgical pinning of his third and fourth fingers. For a whole year, we saw him only on weekends while he attended a rehabilitation facility in Boston, taking the bus there on Sunday nights and returning Fridays to the local pharmacy where we would pick him up. My brother was born about this time, but I don't remember my mother going to the hospital to give birth to him, nursing him, playing with him, or even holding him much. His addition to the family was surely an increased financial burden, and I don't think my mother was adequately prepared to handle the increased stress and responsibilities.

Once my dad finished his rehab, he took a correspondence course on television repair. Just as people love fiddling with computers nowadays, people back then were fascinated by televisions, and being able to repair them was a worthy occupation. If he was gone for the day finding parts for a new project, he always seemed excited to see me when he got home, and if he was sad about losing part of a finger, he never let me know it. He'd make light of his injury by sticking the stub in his nose and making us all laugh.

He was like a big kid. He loved to play games with me and the other kids in the neighborhood. He would let us pitch to him while he called out balls and strikes, and he would forever be the comic when we played basketball in the driveway, pretending not to be able to block our shots and never missing his own. He liked playing just about any board or card game with us, and as we grew older, he would cheat, but he always laughed when we caught him. It became as much fun trying to catch him as it was to win the game.

My first girlfriend was Julie Blanchet. She lived about a block down the street from me, and she loved to play house. I didn't mind as long as I got to play with her piano, an old upright that was set against the stairwell leading up to the second floor. She was pretty, and she liked to draw with bright colorful crayons. She had that distinct girlish way of writing, with curvy letters that seemed to float on the paper while she wrote. In school, Julie was one of our best readers. She was a favorite of the teachers, and I enjoyed competing with her. It was a time in my childhood when it was OK to be one of the smart kids. If the teacher asked a question, I would always try to be the first one to raise my hand, looking for approval when I had the right answer or acknowledgement of being eager if I didn't.

Betty Chandler lived a few houses away from Julie, and the three of us would play together. She was not the scholarly type. She talked rough and was very tomboyish but seemed to like me. She would often chase me around the playground and try to kick me with her pointy black shoes, not necessarily in a hurtful way, but in a way that said, "Please pay attention to me!" Her family was poor, and they lived on the second floor of an old apartment house. Her mother was fat, wore shirts that always seemed too small for her, and smoked a lot of cigarettes.

We had some woods near our house, and I would go off by myself or with others to play in them. I hunted for turtles and snakes, made forts, and played army with my friends in the neighborhood. On one side of the woods was a hill that overlooked Elm Street. In the winter it was a perfect location for throwing snowballs at cars. The county prison was just across the street, but it looked more like a farm with a fence around it than it did a jail. Escapes were common, and when they occurred, the prison siren would sound. Ironically, most people in the neighborhood paid little attention. The convicts were generally not dangerous, and the townspeople, mostly factory workers and laborers, could identify with them. Many people even hoped the convict would get away.

There was a grocery store on the other side of the woods. My friend Jack and I would go there and steal food and comic books. We would hide them in our jackets and take them to our fort where we would read the comic books aloud to each other and feast on the food that we stole.

One day we got caught. We had stolen a couple of sodas and some bananas. We shared them with Julie and Betty, never thinking they'd squeal on us. The next day in school, my first grade teacher asked Jack and me to stay after. Apparently the girls had told her what we did, and the teacher called our parents. I came home that day to my mother crying hysterically, "My son is a thief." I told her that I only stole a five-cent candy bar, lying to her about all the other stuff we'd stolen over the past year, and I agreed to take money from my piggy bank to pay the store manager. The manager accepted it and told me never to steal again. Having been raised Catholic and fearful of eternal damnation, I thought for years that I'd never be able to wipe that "mortal sin" from my slate, and I would surely go to hell someday.

I'm not sure what happened to Betty after grade school, but Julie married a high school football star, got divorced, and remarried. The last I heard, she had about six kids. I saw her at my tenth high school reunion. She remembered the fun times we had as kids, and she still looked pretty good, although I noticed for the first time that one of her front teeth overlapped the one next to it. It's funny that I'd never noticed it when we were younger.

I met Sara Janson in second or third grade. I believe she was the first girl I ever held hands with and probably the first girl I kissed. Her parents owned a Sunoco station on Conway Street, and she lived in an apartment above it. The two of us would often make cookies with her mother, and then we'd spend hours playing the game Cootie Bug, where you'd spin a wheel and try to acquire various plastic body parts, hoping to build your bug first. She had a bean tree in her back yard, and we'd play in it all afternoon sometimes. It was wider than it was tall and had thick horizontal branches, making it easy to climb. As the seasons changed, the bean pods would dry up, turn brown, and fall to the ground. For years after Sara moved away, I would stroll by her house and make note of that tree. As I aged, it seemed to age too. One day, the owner of the station stopped pumping gas, and the air compressor that we used to fill our bicycle tires disappeared. A few years later, the tree was cut down. I guess nothing lasts forever.

From the age of five to about twelve, I didn't think much about gender; I just tried to fit in with the other boys in my neighborhood, playing games like baseball and football, even if I was picked last, which generally was the case. Tim was always one of the captains, and everyone looked up to him. He was the strongest amongst us and generally fair-minded but not someone you wanted to test. The few times I tried, I always ended up on the ground, humiliated, my punches ineffective against the strength and swiftness of his blows. Most times, Tim was protective of me. He wouldn't let the other kids exclude me from the games we played, and because he lived next door, there were many times when just he and I played together.

We played catch, rode our bikes together, bought penny candy and baseball cards whenever we had a little money, and flew kites. We were fascinated by the power of a magnifying glass and its ability to concentrate light, burning leaves and small insects. We would try to catch birds and other small animals using some kind of bait, an overturned box pushed up on one end by a small wooden support, and a string attached to the support that could be pulled to cause the box to fall. It never worked; the box always fell too slowly. We sometimes collected bottles and newspapers from people in our neighborhood, placing them in an old red wagon and pulling it home when it was full. We would store the items in the garage at my house, and when we felt there were enough, we'd cash them in for whatever we could get, often stuffing rocks between the pages of the newspapers to make them weigh more.

Childhood illnesses like measles, mumps, and chicken pox were much more common in those days. It was a time when doctors still made house calls and children were still given small pox vaccinations. I remember Tim getting the measles once and not being able to come out to play. When he finally could come outside again, he was like a war hero, proud that he was selected to have this affliction and pleased to show off the scars of his recently healed sores, as if they were medals he had valiantly won.

I wasn't lucky enough to have measles but instead got mumps—twice. My cheeks were puffed out like a blowfish for over a week, and I remember how painful it was to turn my head or lay my face on my pillow. Unlike measles, when the illness abated, no proof of my fight with this mysterious invader was evident, and there was no envy expressed by the neighborhood kids. I was never special like Tim. No one in our neighborhood was his equal.

The Green River runs through the town of Greenfield. Before I was born, a section of it was dammed and made into a public swimming area with three beaches, a diving board, and a chute. I took swimming lessons there. We all did! It was back in a time when people rarely had their own swimming pools, everyone knew each other, and drive-in movie theaters were still common. The water was always cold but had a freshness to it that was best enjoyed on a really hot day. We would chase minnows, play catch, and if my dad were swimming with us, we'd ride on his back. A concession stand sold ice cream and Fudgsicles. We envied teenagers old enough to be lifeguards, knowing them all by their first names. Sometimes Tim and I would go to the local trucking companies and ask for old tire tubes. We'd patch them and float them down the river from a place called the pumping station, about six miles away. We'd take old broomsticks, tie garden spades to them, and try to spear fish but never with much success.

The pool's not used much anymore. The diving board and the chute are long gone. The refreshment center is closed, and there are no lifeguards at the beaches. The picnic tables are still there, and people play softball and Frisbee in a grassy area near the water on weekends now.

In junior high, when school let out for the summer, many of us worked in the fields for the tobacco companies. They would come to our school and recruit us. They had names like M & M, Culbro, and Consolidated Cigar. During the summer, they would send buses to pick us up around six thirty in the morning and then bring us home shortly after three o'clock. I think we got paid $1.15 per hour, but we could make more doing piecework if we met certain quotas. I typically worked as a picker or a hauler. Picking involved taking the bottom three leaves from each plant, placing the leaves in your lap, scooting down the row, and then placing the leaves to the side for the haulers to pick up. Sometimes we also had to sucker the plants so they would grow bigger leaves. This involved removing small buds forming between the leaves. The plants were supported by nets and bent wires. A string was wound around the top of each plant and attached to the bent wire above. This helped support the plant while it grew. If the straw bosses weren't looking, we would sometimes have dirt ball fights or pull down on a bent wire and wrap one of the strings tighter around the top of a plant so that when you let go, the plant would go flying. When I got home, it would take two baths to get the greenish-brown sticky tobacco juice off my hands.

Girls stayed in the barns helping dry, pack, and sort the tobacco, so we rarely ever saw them. Sometimes we would put frogs or snakes in the hauler's basket, so when the girls received the baskets in the barns, they would get a scare. Madge, who later became my wife, also worked for the tobacco companies in her youth, but it was many years in the future before I had the chance to meet her, and by then the Western Massachusetts tobacco companies had long since abandoned their farms.

I started smoking around age thirteen. We all smoked. We'd go to the park down the street from us in the summer and play baseball all day. It was easy to round up ten to twelve kids to play. We'd sometimes take short breaks to play blackjack, and we'd talk about sports, making dandelion wine, or someone else's parents. It was the thing to do.

Puberty came next, and although it's invariably a difficult time for an adolescent, it was especially difficult for me, because my brain kept trying to tell me that I was female even though my body conveyed the image that I was male.

THE BIRTH OF TWO SELVES

I t's sometimes hard to order events and memories of the past chronologically, as they become meshed, categorized, and distorted with time. I was probably in fifth or sixth grade when I first started secretly wearing women's clothes, often pilfered from the bathroom hamper. I can't remember what made me think to do it for the first time, but I know it excited me, and the excitement perpetuated the behavior. As time went on, I began to develop a second self, and that self would later in my life be known as Jessie. Interestingly, I learned how to isolate and block her temporarily from my mind, possibly to protect myself from feeling insane or being humiliated by her behavior. But it isn't that simple, and I always struggle to explain it. My male and female selves are aware of each other, learn from each other, and respect each other. In later years, my psychologist told me that this is called compartmentalization and common in transgendered individuals.

As a teenager, I grew up in a neighborhood with a lot of other kids my age, and most of us had nicknames. Mark Lacoste had the most. He was called Squint, Keeno, Little Ace, and later just Ace. As for me, I was nick-named Hooter, but sometimes the kids called me Bumpa the Stumpa, in reference to the genital abnormality I was born with. It was cruel, but I had to pretend it didn't bother me so that I wouldn't be picked on.

Adolescence is a time when your abilities and your physical development at age twelve seem to define who you are for the next decade. Whereas I had been reasonably popular in grade school, I struggled in my teens to project any admiration amongst my peers because I lacked masculinity. I was small and was beginning to realize that I was different. My appearance naked was a source of embarrassment. It was easier for me to sit on the toilet rather than to stand. My sex organs were underdeveloped, and I had unusually small breast nipples. When we played sports, I dreaded that my team would be declared "skins," because I didn't want to have to take my shirt off. I stopped showering after gym classes and instead would rush to get my clothes on and get to my next class even if I was sweaty. It was better to be made fun of because you smelled than because you were a sexual misfit.

I had a lot of trouble talking to girls. I became paranoid that they might learn of my sexual inadequacies or how queer my mind worked. I wanted so much to be like them. I would wear panties and my mom's pantyhose to school under my pants. I started painting my toenails, because socks and shoes could hide them. I would wait until everyone was asleep at night, dress in women's undergarments, and then lie under my bed sheets and fantasize how it would feel to be a woman. My female self could not be driven off. As much as I tried, whenever the timing was appropriate and it seemed safe, I found myself unable to hold her back. Jessie wanted so much to live.

The years sixteen to twenty-one are a blur. I did a lot of drugs and drank a lot, hoping that by clouding reality I could be happy. I joined the Air Force when I was seventeen, in part because I didn't feel ready for college, in part because I wanted to escape my hometown, and to a larger extent, because I was trying to conquer this female self within me. I was at odds with this part of me. She hadn't yet become real. She was simply a force inside me that wanted to be adorned, loved color, and was passionate about art and beauty. Throughout the early part of my life, I was constantly reminded these were not the kind of thoughts a man should have. It was not socially acceptable to think this way, yet as much as I tried, I couldn't deny her.

While I was away in Kansas, serving out my enlistment, my brother, five years younger than me, was finishing his senior year of high school and was a varsity starter for the football team. That year his team came in first place and won their division, something no previous team had done in many years. I remember how proud my parents were of him. He was every father's dream. My mom and dad would often call or write to tell me how exciting it was to go to one of his games. They knew every player by his first name, and they met regularly with the other players' parents for pep rallies and after-game parties.

I wanted so much for my parents to be just as proud of me. Joining the Air Force seemed a good means of achieving that goal, but boot camp was horrible. They had community showers in the barracks, and there was no way to avoid exposing my body to other men. I felt like all eyes were on me. In later years, while stationed in Kansas and Texas, living in a dormitory setting, I would wait until late at night to take my shower, when everyone was asleep.

After four years in the service, I returned home. I had an apartment of my own for a short period of time but later found it advantageous financially to move back in with my parents. I made new friends and got back together with some of my old ones. All the while, this woman living inside of me continued to want to express herself. There was always a lot of guilt about secretly coveting this other side of me, but during times of stress, I found comfort in her.

I went off to college, first to the local community college in Greenfield, and then later to Brandeis University in Waltham, Massachusetts. Initially I had no sense of direction as to where to concentrate my studies, and I took classes like art, theater, and oceanography simply because they sounded like they might be fun, but soon I found myself gravitating to those more left-brain academic courses like physics, chemistry, and calculus. I graduated from the community college with highest honors, and my science professor convinced me to try to get into a pre-med program. I applied to a few state schools, and at his suggestion I also applied to Tufts University and Brandeis University. Coming from a small town, I had never heard of Brandeis University, but I remember writing an essay as part of their application process, and I think it was this essay that helped gain my acceptance. The story, still kept in an old filing cabinet, reads like this:

I began walking up the street. A book by Jacques-Yves Cousteau, which I just bought at the used bookstore, was tucked beneath one arm. My other arm swayed along my side. I made the leaves rustle with my feet as I plodded through them. Car wheels were rumbling in the distance.

As I gracefully sauntered up the street, I watched people scurry here and there. Occasionally a passerby and I would share a glance, a nod, or a wince.

I realized how quiet everything was. The bank clock flashed 4:33. I breathed a sigh and look down Main Street. The buildings seemed lifelike as they crouched in the sunset. Their strong backs seemed as if they could hide the town away forever.

A girl's face casually flickered into my thoughts like still shots of a movie. We were splashing in the water together. I could see her smile. I could hear her laugh. I could see her warm eyes and her soft face reflecting what she saw in me. As we splashed in the water, I remember thinking to myself "what a beautiful creature this is". It was as if we were the only two on earth. Even the trees bowed their limbs to us.

The image slowly faded, and I realized how quiet everything really was. I felt a little funny as I gazed up at the sun, its warmth spreading across my face. I closed my eyes and watched the colors illuminated by sunlight. They danced across my face and spun themselves spiraling forever inward.

I opened my eyes, and I could see the huddled buildings once again. The sun was slowly fading. I gripped my book ever so tightly and decided it was time I headed home. Tomorrow would be another day. I was getting hungry, and I felt it getting cold.

When I showed my professor my acceptance letter from Brandeis, he was overjoyed and told me that there was no better choice for me and I had to find a way to go there.

"What was so special about this school?" I thought. "Why haven't I ever heard of it before?" I had heard of the well-publicized universities like Harvard and Yale, but Brandeis? No one in my family had ever been to college, and so my knowledge of higher education was limited. I soon learned of the school's prestige and its long Jewish heritage, but first I had to find a way to afford the tuition.

I applied for every scholarship I could find. The local banks were helpful in this regard as was my guidance counselor at the community college. I worked two full-time jobs the summer before my first semester, applied for loans, and maximized the use of my veteran's benefits. I was determined to make something of myself.

On-campus housing wasn't available to transfer students, so I rented a room with kitchen privileges from an elderly woman a few miles from the school. The room had a bed, a bureau, a desk, and a clothes closet. I could lock the door, and rarely would anyone knock to check on me. The owner of the house rented rooms to a couple of other people too: a girl from Russia who worked in Boston and a guy who was a cab driver. About the only time we ever socialized was when we met in the kitchen for meals. We would have brief conversations, but generally we led pretty separate lives.

At Greenfield Community College, I had been an A-student, graduating with honors, but getting those same grades at Brandeis was not so easy. I was very fortunate to be able to go there, but I was little prepared for the competiveness of the other students. The homework was exhausting, and there never seemed to be enough hours in the day to get it done.

This is probably the time when I first realized how much Jessie could help me. I would come home from school and lock myself in my room, dress as a girl, put make-up on, and magically my homework assignments became much easier to complete.

I enjoyed the privacy I now had to explore this other side of me. I learned to skimp on groceries so I would have money left over at the end of the month to buy female articles of clothing at the downtown department store. Shopping for them was always embarrassing, since men don't usually shop for women's clothing. I would have to make my selections quickly, not like later in life when I was able to spend hours trying on different articles of clothing and scouring every sale rack for bargains. Buying bras, panties, and stockings was the hardest. I worried how the other female customers would perceive me. Standing in line at the checkout counter was agony, especially if it was a long line or if my transaction took any more than a minute or two to complete. I tried to do my shopping around holidays, like Valentine's Day or Christmas, when a man might buy lacy underwear for his spouse or his girlfriend, and I always asked the saleslady for a gift box, pretending I was buying my items for someone else.

From time to time, the guilt and shame I felt about my behavior would consume me, and I would put all my female belongings in a plastic bag and take them to a dumpster. Each time, hoping that I now had the fortitude and the will to put those thoughts out of mind forever, only to find myself saddened by my loss and looking to purchase or steal new items again.

Once, while working with a female graduate student at Brandeis during my senior year, I inadvertently forgot to take all of my eye make-up off, and she noticed. It was the first time anyone had ever caught me, and I felt criminal. I tried to deny the accusation, and she tried to carry on as if it didn't matter, but it was still a humiliating experience.

I felt possessed at times, and even though I loved expressing my feminine side, I felt shameful when I derived sexual pleasure from it. That sort of behavior was considered perverted. No, I needed to be a real girl, and then everything would be OK.

The two years I spent at Brandeis were long and arduous, and I only made a few friendships during my time there, but I graduated in 1984 magna cum laude with honors in biology. I applied to medical school at the University of Massachusetts, but I was unsuccessful in my first attempt.

Figuring I had the summer to be free of responsibility after graduation, I hiked up a path along the high-tension lines near my parents' home, found a spot with good cover, and sunbathed with a woman's two-piece bathing suit on. I did it to get tan marks on my body, ones that I couldn't wash away. I wanted so much to be a girl.

Toward the end of summer, I began interviewing for jobs in Boston. I was looking for a laboratory position that would give me some experience in medical research.

I was offered a position as a technician at Dana Farber Institute in Boston, and I was ecstatic until I learned that I needed to have an employment exam. Then I panicked! What would I do? A medical doctor would surely tell them I had a mental illness if he or she saw those tan marks. I was living with my parents for the summer, and I had already told them how thrilled I was to get the job. What was I going to tell them now? I tried to cover up the marks with self-tanning cream, but it only made them look orange.

I tried sunbathing again, this time in my backyard after my parents went off to work, but the weather wouldn't cooperate; the temperatures were too cool and the skies were overcast. In desperation, I told my dad that working in Boston was too scary for me, that my stomach was in knots, and I couldn't go back there. I asked him to call the research doctor in Boston who wanted to hire me and tell him that the job wasn't right for me. He seemed confused but was respectful of my anxiety. He knew how strong my motivations were, but he also knew that I was insecure at times, and so with some reluctance, he did it. He called the doctor and told him I wouldn't be taking the job.

I eventually did get the tan lines to fade, and later in the fall, I took a job at the Tuft's University Veterinary School, working in their laboratory.

Shortly thereafter, I met Madge, and we fell in love. We met at a football game, and then some months later, we met again at a local tavern and subsequently started dating. We were a good match in the beginning and enjoyed each other's company. I would come home from Boston on weekends, and we would go to movies, go out to dinner, or spend time with our families. I made another attempt to get into medical school at the University of Massachusetts, and with the help of her father, I was accepted.

Madge had plans to go to travel school in Florida; it was a six-month program. I wanted so much for her to stay up north with me, but I knew that if I didn't let her follow her dreams, she would never be happy. I encouraged her to go, and she completed the program. She could have stayed in Florida, but she chose to return and be with me. In the summer between my first and second years of medical school, we were married.

I thought surely marriage would cure me, but it wasn't long before I again started secretly cross-dressing and concealing articles of clothing in an attic crawl space.

During the first year of my residency, at the age of thirty-three, while living in Erie, Pennsylvania, Madge found some women's underwear in a closet. She confronted me and at first suspected I was seeing another woman. I told her that the clothes were mine, and I explained my problem to her. She was more accepting than I thought she'd be. Initially it was awkward for both of us, but we stayed together, and as time went on, as long as my cross-dressing wasn't discussed, it seemed to be something she could live with. In fact, before we had children, I would go up in our spare room after supper, dress in female attire, and read medical journals. Madge would avoid coming up the stairs if she knew I was dressed, but with time she got used to seeing me this way.

I liked clothes that were soft, like turtlenecks with a zipper in the back, knee-high stockings, and gray flannel skirts. Sometimes I liked wearing a dress, but when I did, I would wear thick hose to cover the hair on my legs. My favorite colors were purple, green, and red, no blues back then. I liked heels but not the spiked kind. I was more into a short heel, the kind a woman would wear to work. Scents were important too. I loved the smell of perfumes and became somewhat of a connoisseur of fragrances. As for jewelry, my only choices for earrings at that time were clip-on ones. Most of the styles were big and kind of gaudy. I really preferred small dainty ones. I hated wearing men's rings and rarely wore my own wedding ring. It was not out of disrespect; I just didn't want to wear a man's ring. I wanted to wear diamonds and star sapphires, rubies and emeralds. I wanted to wear pretty necklaces and bracelets with charms. Color was everything to me.

I loved putting on eye shadow and thickening my lashes with mascara. I bought books on how to properly apply make-up and learned that sometimes less was best.

My ideal image of a woman was Audrey Hepburn. I loved thumbing through the Sears catalog and looking at all the latest fashions. I would watch *Easter Parade* with Judy Garland or old Shirley Temple movies over and over again. I wanted so much to be a real girl.

One time my mother-in-law came for a visit and pulled out one of my favorite dresses from a closet. Thinking it belonged to Madge, she decided to wear it to church. I pleaded with Madge not to let her, but there was little either of us could say or do that wouldn't expose the truth about me. It was so upsetting to see her wearing my dress and even worse to learn that she planned to take it home with her. It was months before I got it back.

As time went on, I found myself feeling more and more dishonest about who I was. I could put up a good front when I was with family and friends, but my actions were always guarded. I was in a constant state of apprehension, and I felt like I was always looking over my shoulder for fear that someone might read me.

Our first child was a boy born in Erie, Pennsylvania. We named him Jonathan James Mathewson, because we thought that would be a good professional name, one that we hoped would help him land a well-paying job as an adult. His middle name was his maternal great grandfather's.

In 1992, I accepted a position in family medicine in New Hampshire, where our second child, Adam Guy Mathewson, was born. We thought hard about his name, too, and decided to honor him with Madge's family surname.

When the children were small, Madge often took them to her mother's house on weekends, and I would be left alone to be whoever I wanted to be. As the children got older, though, Madge went away for the weekend less frequently, and I had to be much more careful not to let the children see me dressed.

Travelling out of state for a medical conference was as much a chance to pack my suitcase with dresses and lingerie as it was about taking continuing education courses. For a few days, or sometimes a week, I could let myself be Jessie. She was a prisoner though, confined to a single room in a hotel, and I longed to give her a life of her own with the same freedoms that my male self had.

I got into the habit of wearing panties and women's socks to work, under my trousers that I had hemmed long, taking special care while sitting to avoid having them ride up on my leg. Since these were the only items that I could wear frequently, I had drawers at home stuffed with them.

Up until my forty-eighth birthday, Madge was the only one who knew my secret. By this time in my life, I had seen many patients develop serious medical illnesses, and I watched many of them die, medical science able to do little but delay the event. I sensed my own mortality, and I feared having some catastrophic event like a heart attack occurring at work or a major motor vehicle accident that would leave me helpless and vulnerable to revealing the truth about me.

Something terrible did happen near my forty-eighth birthday but not to me. My father-in-law was diagnosed with gastric cancer and died within months. It all seemed to happen so quickly. At Thanksgiving we were all having a typical dinner together, and he complained that his stomach was bothering him. We all thought he had eaten too much that day. By January, his legs were so swollen with fluid that he couldn't walk, and he was on home oxygen. He had been his high school class president and a Rotarian, and he was a deputy sheriff in the town where he lived. Everyone knew him. He died that winter, and hundreds of people attended his wake, two bishops presided over his church service, and an honor guard stood at attention. I found myself unable to take communion. The self-reproach I felt in regards to my gender conflict had become too much for me to bear.

As a Catholic boy, I grew up believing that sex was shameful to talk about. Around 400 AD, St. Augustine proclaimed that sexual intercourse should occur only between a married man and woman, and the act should take place solely for the purpose of procreation. Any motivations for sex other than that were considered sinful, and no action short of being chaste was pure of heart. The church has implied that philosophy for centuries, and no matter how much people ignore it in practice, it remains ingrained in the minds of many.

As far back as I can remember, I was taught that we are born with original sin. What, then, is original sin? Was Adam's disobedience to God some quantifiable form of defiance, and was I therefore born with some measure of it? As a child, and even as an adult, I have struggled with the meaning of this concept.

Sin seems to have many definitions. One is that it is an act that violates a known moral rule. Who decides what is moral? Growing up in a Catholic family, I often thought about this. Some sins seemed worse than others, and there was always a sense that too much sin would land you in hell, a fiery pit of eternal pain and suffering. Murder, for instance, probably wasn't forgivable unless done as an act of war and with God's permission. Stealing, gambling, indulging in too much drink, or saying a few cuss words in a fit of anger were likely forgivable, but you never knew to what extent.

So what about a man wishing to be a woman? What would the church think of that? The fact that it gave me sexual pleasure when I was young, and the fact that I couldn't deny this part of me (as hard as I tried), left me feeling hopeless. What would it take for God to forgive me? Was there any chance I might find salvation? Would a public confession be enough? How much punishment would I need to endure before I could find God's grace?

It was that dogma that plunged me into a sea of guilt after my father-in-law's death, and it was that guilt that drove me to the brink of suicide.

Now, before proceeding further with this story, I need to regress somewhat, for it was just a few months prior to his death that I was given the privilege of previewing the degree of humiliation I would need to endure if I truly wanted forgiveness.

To accept my penance meant coming to terms with the fact that I might not survive the process.

CRISIS

It was the night the Red Sox won the World Series, October 27, 2004, I believe. I was laying on a gurney in an emergency room, cold and half naked, fearful of my fate.

My career had lost its excitement. The image of the family physician, revered by his patients, devoting his life to the care of the sick, had long since been replaced by the reality of my position: long hours, mountains of paperwork, numerous phone messages to return, and call nights with fragmented attempts to get some sleep. I was constantly trying to find ways to do my job faster and to be more productive. It was assembly line work in a white shirt and tie. Every minute had to be accounted for.

To make matters worse, my physician partner at the time decided she needed to take a two-month leave of absence to stay with her mother, who was very sick and lived in India. I was trying to keep up with the demands of the practice by myself, and I didn't realize how much the stress of my work was affecting me. My back was sore, more so than usual, and I was having abdominal pain. I started having irrational fears. I recalled that my grandfather had colon cancer, and I started to think the worst. I was afraid to eat, and I began losing weight. I didn't have my own personal physician.

I had always diagnosed and doctored myself. This time, I needed someone else's help.

One morning I awoke feeling exceptionally uncomfortable, and I began to panic. I started crying and told Madge that I needed to get to a hospital. I feared going to the local emergency room, because everyone there would know me. I told her that I needed to take the train to Boston where I would be an unknown to the medical providers there. She knew what I feared. I had shaved all the hair off my body and legs, and I had recently tattooed my body in strategic places with numerous butterflies and fairies.

As a young man, my mother would often comment that tattoos were ugly and disgusting. In her mind, only soldiers and convicts got them. The implication was that a professional person would know better. Although they sparked my curiosity, I carried forward my mother's ideals until tattoos became more common to see on women and businessmen. Then I began to think differently about them. As a boy, the ones I typically saw on men exemplified symbols of power, such as a pistol or a dagger, or symbols of vice, such as a half-tipped martini glass or a pair of dice. Later in life, when I decided to get one, I wanted to embrace my feelings of femininity. Originally I planned on getting only one—a small, pretty butterfly. I had it placed just below my belt line, where it wasn't easily visible, and I must tell you that it was both sexually gratifying and somewhat seductive to know it was there and to know it was permanent. By getting that first one without discussing it with Madge, I had elected to exclude her from the mutual decision-making process that normally takes place between married couples. In a way, I was unfaithful to her. Before long, I had many more.

Madge hesitated over going to the hospital with me but then agreed to go. In the early part of my transition, she was generally supportive; although in retrospect, I suspect she was in denial to the reality of what was happening to me. I, on the other hand, no longer able to live a life of self-reproach, was forcing my destiny.

I had wanted this day to come for some time. A midlife crisis is a cliché until you have one. Feeling that my life was more than half over, I felt I needed to confess and tell the world the truth about me before it was too late. I couldn't let myself die so shamefully, with no chance of God's forgiveness.

I called my office manager and in a desperate tone of voice told her that I was sick and needed to go to the hospital. She must have sensed my anxiety, because she said, "Do what you need to do. We can rearrange your schedule."

About two hours later, after taking the train to Boston with Madge, I arrived at Beth Israel Hospital. I told the triage nurse that I was worried I might have an abdominal obstruction and feared something ominous might be the cause. She acknowledged my concern but didn't look alarmed. She took my vitals and put me in the waiting room, where I think I sat some seven hours before I was finally called and brought into an exam room. After about the fifth hour, I sent Madge home, because I didn't want our kids, who were only young teenagers, to come home from school and find no one there. She didn't want to leave me, but we both knew it was best for her to go.

I had my PDA with me, an electronic note taker of the time, and with nothing else to do, I wrote the following letter to my family, just in case my worst fears became a reality.

To Madge,

I love you. You've always been there for me. Forgive me for the times I've spoken harsh toward you. Remember me for the good things I've done.

To Jonathan,

I love you. You can do great things with your life. You have many talents. Learn to control your temper, be more forgiving of others, and learn compassion. Your ability to problem solve is one of your greatest strengths (I think you inherited this from me).

To Adam,

I love you. Your greatest strength is your sensitivity. It can create deep emotions that can sometimes be overwhelming to the human spirit, but it can also be potentially very rewarding. You may have to work harder than others to achieve your goals, but I have faith in you.

As for me, I've lived a good life. No regrets. I did think I'd live longer but that's OK. I hope God will accept me.

Once in the exam room, a nurse had me take off all of my clothes and put a Johnny on. There was no door, just a curtain, and the bed had only one sheet. I hadn't eaten all day, because I was afraid I might need to go to surgery, and I felt lightheaded and dizzy. I was so embarrassed and feared that people would soon be talking about me. I kept staring at the curtain, knowing any minute a doctor would come in. I felt my time was just about up, and I had to come clean.

Just then an intern walked in the room. He was pleasant but obviously inexperienced. I thought to myself, "If I forewarn him about my appearance, before he lifts the sheet, and if I say the right words to explain myself, maybe he'll be compassionate." He moved to my bedside and proceeded to ask me questions about my medical history, as I expected he would.

Then the moment of truth came. He was ready to examine me. I was fearful of what he might think. Looking forlorn, I said to him, "Please don't judge me. I'm not a bad person. Really I'm not." He lifted the sheet, stared at my exposed body for a few seconds, and then tried not to alter his facial expression. I felt I was at the gallows, hoping the executioner would pardon me. Where had life's journey taken me? Was this really happening? I lay paralyzed for a moment, wondering if time was going to stand still. I took a breath to reassure myself that it hadn't and watched as my examiner seemed to take a moment to collect himself and then acknowledge that he needed to be nonjudgmental.

"I'm not sure what might be causing your discomfort," he remarked, "but I'll order some tests, and the attending physician will be in shortly."

A little while later, his supervising physician did come into the room. Likely forewarned, he too lifted the sheet to examine me, saw my perversity, and said in a somewhat sarcastic way, "So you're a physician?"

"Yes" I said. "I think I have an abdominal obstruction. Please don't judge me by the way I look."

I handed him my medical history that I had typed up some time ago and had stored on my computer. He looked at it, didn't say much, did a less-than-thorough exam, and rather indignantly said he'd order a CT scan. He left the room, and I never saw him again. I felt like street trash. I was a GOMER, an acronym sometimes used by ER doctors to mean Get Out of My Emergency Room. Being in the city, he'd probably seen many people like me. I was so blind to the reality that I was a transsexual. I cringed at the word transvestite, a term I associated with black stockings and garter belts, spiked heels and rouge. Although I had worn those things on occasion, I wanted more. I wanted to be a real woman, to smell nice, to look pretty, to wear the latest fashions, and to have no one suspect that I had actually been born a male.

While I was waiting for the results of my tests, I could hear cheering. The Red Sox were winning, and they would soon be the World Series champions. I kept asking my nurse, "What inning is it? Who's at bat? What's the score now?" After the game ended, she came in to my room elated and told me crowds were gathering near Fenway. I wanted so much to be a part of the excitement, and I couldn't help but feel I was being cheated of a celebration I had waited years for. There was nothing I could do though, and in later years, I would mark that day as the possible beginning of my transition.

I drifted off to sleep sometime after midnight, only to be awakened a few hours later by a different intern who was staring at a copy of my CT scan report. He looked up briefly at me and said rather indignantly, "You have to go home!"

"But I'm sick! Isn't there something wrong with me?"

"Your CT scan is normal. You probably have irritable bowel syndrome. Here's a copy of your report. You should try to get more fiber in your diet. You must know that!" Then he left. He just turned and walked out without any desire or attempt at discussion. At first I felt dumbfounded; then I realized what he said was true. My symptoms were the result of stress, nothing organic. It was a diagnosis I had made myself to countless patients through the years, discounting and dismissing it as a psychological problem. Now I understood. How could I have been so blind to my own diagnosis?

I packed my things, left the ER, and groped through the lonely dark streets of Boston in early morning. I was lost in the comprehension of what had happened. Eventually I found a subway entrance and caught the Lowell commuter train home. I called Madge and asked her to pick me up at the station. How would I explain all this to her? I had her convinced, as I had convinced myself, that I was deathly ill. Would she be sympathetic when I explained that I didn't have a physical illness, but rather I was mentally unwell? I had missed a diagnosis that was most obvious to me now. How could that have happened? What would I tell my office staff?

I needed a medical professional, a doctor of medicine or psychiatry whom I could confide in. I couldn't let this happen again. Where was I going to find such a person?

FINDING A CONFIDANT I
COULD TRUST

I met Dr. Gransby at a family medicine conference in Vermont about a month after my father-in-law died. She was seated in the auditorium in front of me, and we talked casually between lectures. She was tall, had long brownish-blond hair, was dressed in slacks, and had a small black purse with a purple lining that you could carry like a knapsack. I was attracted to the shape of her face and the way she squinted with her glasses on. Her mannerisms and the way she walked suggested she was a little clumsy at times, but maybe that's what appealed most to me. The placard in front of her indicated her name was Donna Gransby, and she worked in Lebanon, New Hampshire, the home of Dartmouth College.

"Could she be the one?" I thought to myself. "She seems like someone I might be able to confide in." I was in desperate need of a physician, and I felt it had to be a female who could empathize with me. If I didn't find someone soon, I could foresee eventually ending up in another horrible predicament like the humiliation I endured four months previously in the emergency room in Boston. The conference ended with her having no knowledge that I was planning to make an office appointment with her, but I had made my decision; she would be the one.

A few months later, I met with her to discuss some back pain I was having. Although this was a legitimate complaint, I was also trying to find out if I could comfortably speak to her about my gender conflict, whether by my own volition or forced circumstances. My experience at Beth Israel Hospital had given me some sense of the worst possible outcome. In order for her to examine me, I had to at least let her see a tattoo of a fairy on my lower back.

Before undressing, I showed her my tie that had a miniaturized picture of Walt Disney standing against an open door with a keyhole in the shape of Mickey Mouse in the background. I wanted to know if she had an appreciation for art and how intuitive she was. I asked her who was pictured on the tie. Most people I had asked this question of missed the implication of the keyhole and failed to make the connection but not her. She got it right away.

She was sitting not too far from me as I undressed to my underpants and lifted the back of my tee shirt. I stood waiting for her reproach but instead her facial expression changed little, and she simply asked me to step closer to her so she could examine me. I looked sheepishly toward her and was trying to think of what to say when she said, "It doesn't matter, don't worry about it."

Don't worry about it! Who was this person? She pressed on my spine and lower back, but she didn't feel compelled to have me fully undress. Was it fate that I had found her? She was so beautiful to me. I memorized her smile, the sound of her voice, and the way she furrowed her brow, but I sensed it was not yet time to tell her everything. She was too focused on my complaint of back pain today, and the visit was not intended to be a long one. What I had to tell her couldn't be rushed. She had accepted me so far without question, and that was enough for now.

She ordered some x-rays and told me a little about herself, including the fact that she was divorced, remarried, and born a year before me. I wanted to know so much more. I could sense she knew I was struggling with my marriage and was mindful of the possible outcome, but she distanced herself to avoid false prediction. In this regard, she and I shared a common bond.

Madge was a wonderful person, but we had been growing apart for some time. We had been married almost sixteen years. When we were young, I loved her because she believed in me and accepted me like no other woman had before. For her part, I was the image of success: someone who could be a good provider, faithful to her and our children, and someone who could be a pillar of the community we lived in, like her dad had been. Her father had been a prominent member of the Episcopalian church, a star football player during his high school years, and everyone in town knew who he was. Madge and I had a good arrangement, but as time passed, intellectually I was losing interest. She was not a scholar. She was a pragmatist and a devoted Catholic. She was a good mother but a terrible cook. She was a friend to everyone she met, but her ability to conceptualize with me was limited. I couldn't talk to her about abstract topics or theories that had no clear answer. She preferred conversations that were more concrete. We went to church on Sunday, because we were taught as children that if we didn't go, we wouldn't find salvation. It didn't matter whether we wanted to be there or not; it was an obligation. She couldn't imagine life as just existence or that there might not be an afterlife. She respected authority, and even if she didn't totally agree with something her father or mother said, she felt it disobedient to question them.

I could relate to Donna in a way that had never been possible with Madge. She was a physician like me. Maybe it was her body language, but I could tell she kept an open mind about what people confided to her. She owned her own practice, a rare feat in these times. I could sense her compassion and the ability to empathize with her patients. I knew she was different. She was a little bit of a rebel like me, and I knew she would treat me well. As I left her office, I scheduled another appointment and requested a longer visit. I had to wait a few weeks to see her again, but fortuitously I was given the last appointment of the day.

In those weeks before my next visit, I planned how I would tell her what I had never confided to anyone before, not even Madge. I wouldn't have much time. All my life I had dreamed of being a woman. How would I explain this to her in thirty minutes? I decided to appeal to her sensitivity and wrote a story about my life, revised many times over, and mailed it to her a few days before my visit. I could only hope that I'd found the right words.

TIME TO TELL

It was my birthday. I was born a Gemini, the twin sign. It was no more a choice for me than it was to deny it suited me.

Dr. Gransby knocked first on the examining room door and then opened it. She was carrying a manila envelope in her arms, propped as if to say she still remembered her schoolgirl days. She smiled, greeted me, and then acknowledged that she enjoyed reading my story. She took a seat, and we contemplated where to begin.

Prior to my arrival, I had rehearsed this visit a hundred times over, and the fictional ending always came out different, sometimes bad, sometimes good. In one of the endings, Dr. Gransby handed me a gun and said, "OK, if you're not happy, shoot yourself," while in another I found myself walking through the woods with her, discussing philosophy. What actually happened was more beautiful than anything I imagined.

I had written to her about my childhood, how I had struggled for acceptance in my teens, and how I felt sexually inadequate. I told her about my surgeries, the one I had as a child and the one I had later in my twenties.

I was born with a combination of genital defects that are estimated to occur one in every fifteen hundred births. Interestingly, the incidence of these birth defects has been increasing over the past few decades, suggesting an environmental influence. The cause of them may be related to a deficiency of prenatal andro-gens. It is a fact that the brain has an abundance of sex hormone receptors, and one can theorize that the effects of estrogen and testosterone influence brain development. Since the testes develop in the first trimester and the brain in the third, one can further theorize that it's possible for the brain to be sexed differently than what's suggested by one's gonads.

Although I could no longer remember details of the first surgery, and relied instead on what my parents told me, the second was still vivid in my mind.

My thoughts drifted back to a time when I was an airman stationed in the Midwest. On occasion, when I was sick, I would go to the infirmary. The medical provider there was neither an officer nor a physician, but he had a gentle disposition and seemed respectful of me. He was very knowledge-able. On one particular visit, he correctly diagnosed a certain skin malady I had acquired and prescribed an effective treatment. I felt I could trust him. One day I decided to ask him if he knew of anything that could be done to help me. I told him of my difficulties using the toilet. I was convinced that if I could just get this problem fixed, the intrusive thoughts I had daily of wanting to be a woman would go away.

There was an awkward moment letting him examine me, but he took my concern seriously and arranged for me to go by commercial airlines to Wilford Hall Medical Center in Texas, the largest Air Force hospital in the country. I was admitted to the urology unit, where a young surgeon greeted me and took me to a small room where he asked me to lower my pants. He inserted probes to measure the opening of my urethra and then grabbed a large camera. He told me about a new surgical procedure he was trying that he described as a flap repair. He was polite but seemed more interested in how the success of the opera-tion would benefit him as opposed to me. He advised me that he was going to take some pictures.

I eyed him suspiciously. "What for?"

"For a medical journal that I hope to publish the results in," he replied.

I didn't like this proposal. People would see me naked, and the defor-mity that had caused me so such embarrassment all my life would be out there for everyone to see.

Sensing my concern, he remarked, "Don't worry. No one will know it's you. We'll block out your face."

I still didn't like it, but what choice did I have? I took a moment to contemplate my options. If I refused, I'd probably never get another chance to have this corrected. Why should I care if they put my picture in some obscure journal? No one I knew would ever read it. Besides, he said they'd block my face.

I don't know if his research or that picture was ever published. At the time, I didn't care to know. He was an officer, and I was an enlisted man with a high school education. I knew nothing about medicine at the time and thought only about how I might meet a girl and fall in love. I had no experience with sexual intercourse and feared that I would not perform well. I longed to be "normal" like everyone else.

So there I was, some twenty-five or so years later, addressing the same dilemma with Dr. Gransby. The previous surgeries had not bestowed upon me a cure. I still felt sexually inadequate, and I still had these constant obsessions about wearing female clothing and imagining myself as a woman.

Dr. Gransby proceeded to ask me some additional questions about my medical history, and she suggested the problem I was having was similar to that of women with small breasts. I recognized that there was some validity to her statement, and I appreciated her empathy, but I was struggling with something much more powerful and innate than either of us understood at the time. It was my gender identity.

I was so confused. Why was I having these thoughts? What was wrong with me? Wasn't there something someone could do to help me? Was I destined to struggle forever on my own with this problem? Somehow I knew Dr. Gransby could help me. I felt God had predetermined us to meet.

I pulled three pictures out of a canvas bag. Two were Norman Rockwell prints, and the third was from an unknown artist. Each had its own meaning. I placed them down separately on the desk between us. Dr. Gransby took a moment to study each. The first was of a young girl sitting in a chair, staring into a mirror, a book draped in her lap, and open to a page showing a fashionable woman. The second was of a teenage girl wearing a red sweater and skirt, running headlong with an easel tucked under one arm and carrying a paint box and canvas in the other. The third was of a woman sitting on a ledge with her eyes closed, small fairies hovering around her. When I was sure she'd had enough time to absorb their meaning, I shifted my gaze in her direction. She looked a little perplexed, unsure of her sense of intuition, and hesitated to respond.

"These pictures, Dr. Gransby, they're pictures of me." I started to cry and proceeded to unbutton my shirt a little, exposing a lavender camisole I was wearing. I pulled it to the side some and further revealed to her a tattoo of a beautiful butterfly and my pretty opal necklace, also in the shape of a butterfly. I could see in her face the look of astonishment and temporary insecurity as she took a moment to compose herself. As for me, I could no longer hold back the tears.

"I don't know why I feel this way, Dr. Gransby! I don't know what to do! I like these things, but I know I'm not supposed to."

She took a moment to consider her answer, looked at me compassionately rather than with contempt, and told me it was OK to feel the way I did. It didn't make me any less of a person, and it didn't mean I was evil. I just had a strong feminine side. In her words, I had more yin than yang.

I wept, and on that day, I turned and faced the monster that had been chasing me for so many years. It could have killed me—I knew that—but instead it stood powerless, naked along life's path, stripped of its enormous strength, and no longer able to hurt me. Although it was something I imagined, Dr. Gransby seemed impervious to its mighty force, and in my mind she simply told it to leave and never try to harm me again. It yielded to her demand, because it had no influence over her, and with her help it faded from my imagination like a bad dream. From then on, I would forever be grateful to her for her willingness to help me.

As if I somehow knew that our meeting would be favorable, I brought a couple of gifts for her. From my bag, I handed her a Hilary Duff compact disc, appealing to young girls, and a small fairy figurine wrapped in pretty paper. Jessie was in a sense a child at this time. She existed in my mind, I knew her name, but she had not yet had any true-life experiences of her own. Dr. Gransby gave her permission to come out from hiding, to explore the world around her, and to experience all that life could offer. Like a metamorphosis, everything would soon change. My female self was no longer confined to my imagination, and Dr. Gransby would become Jessie's first real friend.

For most people in New England, May 24, 2005, would be remembered as a cold, damp, rainy day. But for me, it was bright and sunny, with rainbows, and white birds chirping. I was about to start a new life, a "do over" as some might say. It was a time to relish the moment and thank God for hearing my prayers. Little could I realize how monumental and difficult the changes ahead would be for me, but for now, everything was new and beautiful.

BEGINNING THE TRANSITION

I became obsessed with meeting Dr. Gransby again. After learning she would be attending a medical conference sponsored by the Dartmouth Medical Center, I enrolled in the course as well. I rented a hotel room the night before in Lebanon, New Hampshire, only to find out the next day that the conference was actually in Manchester, less than twenty miles from my home. How could I have done that? I had travelled over two hours to stay overnight in the wrong city!

As I drove frantically back to Manchester, I started to panic. I couldn't breathe. Something inside of me was evolving, affecting my thoughts. I was fearful of it, but likewise, I didn't want to repress it. It was my female self, my alter ego. I felt I was losing control. I had to pull my car over to the side of the road. Acting on impulse and knowing I was being irrational, I called Dr. Gransby's office hoping to get a message to her.

Her nurse answered. "Dr. Gransby's office, can I help you?"

I hesitated. "Hi, this is Jessica Birch. Is it possible for me to speak with Dr. Gransby?"

"I'm sorry, she's not in today. She has the day off. Can I take a message?"

Of course she had the day off. I knew that. She was at the conference. "I need help! I'm shaking, and I can't concentrate. I'm worried that I can't drive my car."

I sensed concern in her voice. "Do you want me to have the covering physician call you back?"

I took a moment to contemplate a response. It all seemed surreal. "No. I'd rather not speak with anyone else. I think I can wait. I'm better now. I'll be OK."

"Are you sure?"

I wasn't sure of anything anymore, but I only wanted to talk with her. "Yes, I'm sure. I'll be OK. Really! Can you have her call me tomorrow?"

There was still time to get to the conference before it ended. I had to see her, to talk to her again, but I wasn't thinking clearly. How would I explain my phone message? I'd figure something out. I just needed to get there.

I arrived at the conference in the middle of a lecture, checked the program pamphlet, and saw Dr. Gransby's name listed. I found a seat in the back and scoured the lecture hall for her. She wasn't there! Where was she?

The next day, she called me at work. I told her what had happened to me the day before, how I saw her name on the conference roster, and wondered why I hadn't seen her. I told her how I had panicked on the highway and had to pull my car over. Naive of my insanity, she remarked, "It was too nice a day to be cooped up inside, so I stayed home. You need to see someone else besides me, a psychologist. I don't know how to help you."

My mind went blank. Sadness filled my thoughts. What was I going to do?

Dr. Gransby proceeded to converse further with me. "I had a patient once who thought she had multiple personalities, and her psychologist was very helpful. There's also someone at Dartmouth you might find helpful. Let me see if I can find their names."

She gave me the names of a couple of people, but I could tell that she had no idea if they were knowledgeable about gender disorders. I acknowledged that I appreciated her help and went back to seeing my own patients.

A day or two later, I called a psychologist in Nashua who I had known for many years. Pretending I was responding more to duty than concern,

I told him I had a patient confused about his gender and wondered if he knew of anyone who might be able to help him. He advised me that he'd ask some of his colleagues and try to get back to me.

I really wasn't expecting him to find anyone, so I was surprised one day when my receptionist interrupted me during a patient visit to say he was on hold and that he was asking to speak with me. I excused myself from the exam room and went to my office to take the call.

"Hi, Jacob? I'm calling you about that patient with the gender disorder you asked me about. I found a doctor by the name of Alice Braunwald who might be of help to you. She works in Concord. Do you want her number?"

Of course I did, but I had to contain my excitement and try not to sound too enthusiastic. I indicated to him that I was making note of it and acknowledged that I appreciated his help.

Later in the day, when I had a break, I left her a message and heard back shortly after.

"Hello, Dr. Mathewson? I'm returning your call. Is there something I can do to help you?"

That was a loaded question! Feeling it best to not yet reveal my true intentions, I replied, "Yes, Dr. Braunwald, I think there may be. I have this patient struggling with some issues about his gender. I'm not sure how to help him. Is this the kind of patient you see in your practice?"

"It is. Would you like me to see him?" she asked. "What's his name?"

I hesitated. How should I continue? It made no sense to keep on pretending. "Dr. Braunwald," I paused for a moment, "this patient—it's me." Near nausea took hold of me. Oh my God, what had I just said?

The tone of her voice changed to better suit the conversation.

"I see!" A short silence occurred, and then she said, "Would you like to see me next Tuesday at 2 p.m.?"

Caught off balance, I took a moment to think. That was my afternoon off. That would work! I was having trouble understanding so many things. She might be the bridge, the conduit I needed to navigate through my mind and make order out of all the turmoil.

I felt both anxious and relieved. "OK then," I said. "Tuesday at 2 p.m. it is. Thank you. I'll see you then."

MEETING MY THERAPIST

Since the time of my childhood, I had been taught that transvestites and transsexuals were sexually deviant people. The torment I lived with every day stemmed from my own sense of association with this group mixed with constant denial. It created a sort of schism in me; one part thirsted for more knowledge and the other feared what it might find. When I researched this topic at the library, I would go when no one else was around, so that I could read in seclusion. My endeavors were vastly disappointing. I either didn't know how to research this topic, or I read all of the wrong books. What little information I could find discussed these individuals in the context of a mental illness. If a person felt they were born in the wrong body, experts advised psychotherapy so that the patient could become more comfortable with the sex they were assigned at birth.

I arrived at Dr. Braunwald's office a little early. There was only one patient in the waiting room, a young man with shoulder-length blond hair. I knew he was a man because he had large hands, a wide jaw, and a receding hairline, but I couldn't help notice that he also had breasts and rather large ones too. I surmised I was in the right place.

I took a seat and noticed Dr. Braunwald's door was ajar. Since we were both medical professionals, I never gave it a thought that it might be improper to walk over, knock on her door, and say hello without a formal invitation. Right from the start, she made it clear to me that there were boundaries, and I had just crossed one. With some assertion of authority, she advised me to take a seat in the waiting room. She would come get me when she was ready.

I felt hurt and humiliated. I wasn't used to being treated that way. Still, I took my seat and contemplated my role. Several minutes later, as if part of her usual routine, she came out and asked, "Are you Dr. Mathewson?" After confirming that I was, she continued, "I'm Dr. Braunwald. Will you come with me?" And she escorted me back to her office.

As I stepped in the room, I was quick to notice that there was a couch and chair unoccupied, just like I'd seen on TV and in the movies. I chose the chair, and after a brief silence, she initiated the conversation. "So, Jacob, what brings you here today?"

I glanced around the room and noticed that she liked plants. She was an older woman, in her mid-to late-fifties, had a sort of beatnik look, and wore sandals with socks. I wasn't sure what to tell her first.

"Dr. Braunwald, I don't know why I wear these glasses," pointing to my women's frames.

I had bought them at a local optical store, pretending they were for a friend so that the sales lady wouldn't think they were for me. Then I sent them by mail, along with my prescription, to a company in Texas where the lenses could be made. Their feminine appearance was subtle enough that I could get away with wearing them at work.

Next, I showed her my socks. Only by lifting my pants could someone tell which gender they were made for. Still waiting for her reprove, I showed her my butterfly tattoo. I was expecting her to ask me questions about possible motivations for my female inclinations, but instead she nodded in affirmation and blurted out, "You're transgendered!"

"Transgendered? What does that mean?" I asked, ignorant of the term.

She twisted her face and narrowed her eyes as if to say, "You've surely heard of this? You're a physician, aren't you?" But I'd never heard the term.

She took a moment to realize that I was genuinely perplexed, and then she proceeded to explain. "Some people enjoy wearing clothes of the opposite sex, and some even feel they should have been born the opposite sex. People like this are called transgendered. There's nothing wrong with having these feelings. You don't have an illness. It's just that your gender identity is female."

I looked at her bewildered. "Do you mean I'm not sick? I don't understand."

She chose her words carefully. "Gender identity is something you're born with. You don't choose it. In some cultures people like yourself are highly revered for their knowledge of both sexes. They're called Shaman, a sort of tribal medical doctor."

"Wait a minute!" I said. "Are you telling me that I don't need to feel guilty about myself, that it's OK to feel the way I do? I'm not a bad person?"

Her voice sounded somewhat maternal. "That's right. It's not wrong to feel the way you do. It's just the way you are. Do you have a female name?"

She caught me off guard. How did she know this? "It's...it's Jessica," I replied.

Thinking back, I vaguely remember experimenting with other names, but at some point Jessica stuck. I created an image of her in my mind, and I let her take on a character of her own. I used this name as my computer password at work, and sometimes I ordered things through the mail as Jessica Birch—catalogs and stuff, things women usually like to get. I didn't want the companies to think I was male.

"How long have you been cross-dressing?" she inquired.

I hesitated to answer, but I was starting to feel more at ease and safe with her. "Since fifth or sixth grade I think. It's just been going on so long...I've tried to stop, but I can't."

"Have you ever thrown your things away?"

She really did have some expertise in gender disorders! Only someone specially trained would know to ask this question. Many times in the past, like an addict hoping to give up their habit, I would pack up all of my female garments, jewelry, and make-up for the trash, depositing them in the woods or a dumpster somewhere, only to find myself a week later acquiring new ones. "I'm so ashamed of the way I think sometimes. I've done this many times, but I'm weak. I always end up collecting them again. I feel so helpless to resist."

"That's called purging, a common behavior in those who are transgendered. You're feeling ashamed of who you are but you shouldn't." She suggested I read a book called *True Selves*, and we continued to talk for close to an hour. I was amazed at how well she already knew me.

Toward the end of the visit, I asked, "Do you have other patients like me?"

She just grinned. "A good portion of my practice is transgendered. I have many patients like you. Do you want to come back and see me again in two weeks?"

THE PROCESS BEGINS

My journey had begun, and my sessions with Dr. Braunwald soon became routine. I hungered for knowledge, and she became my mirror, my Yoda, helping me see what I had never been able to see before. At various times, I would be the student, the victim, the fool, and the crusader. I began reading everything I could find on the subject of gender identity and what it meant to be transgendered.

With her help, I learned to accept who I was. With each visit, I felt more enlightened and less insecure. Like peeling an onion, the removal of each layer helped me see the origins of the one before it. With knowledge came change, and the more I learned, the more I felt myself wanting to be a different person.

Hormone therapy is an integral component of a transsexual's transition to the opposite sex. The World Professional Association for Transgender Health provides guidelines for physicians and therapists regarding the medical care of transsexuals. These were originally written by Dr. Harry Benjamin, one of the first physicians to provide hormone treatments to transsexuals and best known for his association with Christine Jorgensen, the now famous and highly publicized transsexual of the 1950s. These guidelines recommend a minimum of three months of psychotherapy before consideration of hormone therapy. I broke that rule, but not knowingly at the time.

Long before I started seeing Dr. Braunwald, I had been intermittently taking birth control pills from the office, unsupervised, knowing that their estrogen content could cause my breasts to develop. I took them in the same way an alcoholic took "just one more drink," always telling myself that this would be the last time. As my therapy progressed and I became aware of the guidelines, generally referred to as the Harry Benjamin Standards of Care, I learned that taking hormones was an expected part of the transition process although not obligatory. My self-reproach soon became transformed into jubilation, although clearly the way I had been taking hormones was misguided and premature. In time, Dr. Gransby would prescribe them for me and supervise my treatment. My regimen would consist of a daily birth control pill in conjunction with an estrogen patch. Although this is not a typical formula, it is the one I chose after consultation with her, and it has worked well for me.

Getting patients to lose weight is often more difficult than curing cancer, yet my weight went from 210 pounds down to 142 in a little over a year. I'd never had the willpower to lose weight before. How was this possible? I'm not sure, but I have a theory. It's a known scientific fact that our body weight changes little from day to day. This is because there's an area in the brain called the hypothalamus that works at keeping our weight near a certain set point. It does this by controlling our hunger and manipulating our basal metabolic rate. A similar process regulates our body temperature. The hypothalamus is thought to relay messages in some way to a central command area of the brain that has the ability to modify that set point.

What if my sense of having two selves, one male and one female, is really based in biology? If my female self was becoming dominant, might my brain now be obliged to follow a different set of instructions? My food tastes were changing. I found myself craving pickles and olives when I'd hardly ever eaten them before. Vegetable dishes were now more appealing, and I found myself eating less and still feeling full. In fairness to other possibilities, I was taking medications for depression as well as hormones, and I was exercising more. All these things, I'm sure, had their effect on me.

The costs associated with a gender change are phenomenal, and I was soon to learn just how expensive that would be, but I was also fortunate, unlike most transsexuals, I had the financial resources to make it all possible. Laser hair removal was the first step in the process. At Dr. Braunwald's suggestion, I started making visits to a spa in Concord that was familiar with the needs of transgendered clients and happy to work with them.

The light energy from a laser is highly effective in destroying pigmented hairs in the growth phase. White or unpigmented hairs, blond hairs, or hairs in the resting phase cannot be treated. For this reason, it's typically offered as a series of treatments for various body areas at a package cost. Generally, an area like the face, could cost $1000 or more. Hairs untreatable would need to be removed permanently with electrolysis, a much more painful and arduous process.

Madge actually came with me to one of my first treatments in Concord. I was nervous going there. I wasn't sure how the people at the spa would treat me. In the past, without her knowledge, I had gone to Boston and had my arms lasered, but back then it was under the guise that I was just a man who didn't want hairy arms. Here, they knew I was transgendered. What I was asking for would permanently change my appearance.

The cosmetologists were all very nice to me, and as time went on, I got to know many of them on a first-name basis. Madge chose to take a neutral stance with me over those treatments in the beginning. I don't think she was ready to separate from me; she hoped that by allowing me to proceed, I would see that she still cared for me, and then I would stop going. She knew I was seeing Dr. Braunwald every week or every other week, and I think she believed that whatever I was going through was temporary, and with the help of a psychologist, I would regain my senses. Maybe Madge saw Dr. Braunwald as an authority figure and trusted her judgment. Her father had taught her to respect people of authority, and she would never go against his wishes. However, I thought differently. Although I enjoyed my visits with Dr. Braunwald and valued her opinion, I was headstrong in my desire to fully transition, and I wanted it to happen as quickly as possible. No object in my way could halt my progress. Eventually I sacrificed my relationship with Madge for what I deemed to be self-preservation. I often feel sad about that choice, and although I later argued that I did it because I couldn't deny my gender identity, it caused me to lose the one person who loved me more than any other at the time.

No longer shackled by guilt, and not yet feeling blame for the deterioration of our marriage, the changes in me started to proceed at a rather reckless rate, and in some ways I was like a runaway train. One day at work, I wrote a letter to Dr. Gransby, whom I now felt comfortable addressing as Donna, and told her about a new women's road bicycle that Madge reluctantly agreed to let me buy. It was a light blue color and not obviously feminine, but all that mattered to me was that I knew it was built for a woman. I also told her about things I had been discussing with Dr. Braunwald. I made a photocopy of the letter and mailed it to her. I'm not sure if I did it subconsciously with purpose, or whether it was truly accidental, but I left the original letter in the office photocopier and went home.

The next day my receptionist found the letter and questioned me about it. I wasn't sure what to tell her. We had known each other for some time, and I didn't feel I could lie to her.

"I'm seeing a therapist. I'm trying to work through some things that have been bothering me for a while."

Rather than chastise me, she seemed more worried that I would perceive her actions as an intentional intrusion into my affairs.

"I didn't know what it was! I thought it was something related to the practice. I read it so I'd know what to do with it!" She took a moment to observe my reaction and then proceeded to tell me, "I was brought up in New Jersey. These things don't bother me."

I was thankful for her understanding and went back to my work.

SEX, GENDER, AND
METAMORPHOSIS

Ambivalent! It's the way I often feel. It's being happy and sad at the same time, determined to be who I want to be but realizing the cost will be great and just hoping to have enough fortitude to complete the journey. Jessie makes me happy. I can close my eyes, imagine her, and thus become her. The sadness relates to all the heartache associated with her development (Journal entry October 11, 2005).

After meeting Dr. Braunwald and learning that becoming the opposite sex was not an insurmountable task, my desire to become female was so intense that it obscured my ability to think clearly about its consequences. I cared little about how my actions might impact others. This was my life, and I was determined to live it the way I wanted to. People would just have to adjust. What I failed to appreciate though was that for every step I took forward, those who loved me felt a loss. Not yet having experienced a prolonged grief reaction myself, I had no sense of the sadness other people must have felt. Dr. Braunwald, or Alice as I came to know her, tried desperately to slow me down, but I was so excited about the changes occurring in me that I often didn't give myself enough time to process her advice. It wasn't that I didn't listen; it's just that her effect on me was not always immediate, and by the time I was able to grasp what she was trying to tell me, it was too late and I had already caused myself hardship or hurt someone close to me.

She suggested that the people in my workplace should be the last to know of my intentions. Instead, they were some of the first people I told. She encouraged me to focus on cosmetic issues that weren't immediately noticeable to others, like hair removal, which was a slow, gradual process. Instead, after piercing one ear, I chose to display a beautiful, jeweled, butterfly earring and started coloring my hair.

It's been said that old friends know you best because they can see who you are and they know where you've been. I often wonder if our lives are predetermined. What if everyone we meet, every experience we share with others, every idea or concept that's formed in our minds has some grand purpose?

Not a day goes by that I don't relive parts of my transition. Why was it so important for me to make this change? What if I truly understood just how hurtful my actions might be to others? Would I still have made the same choices?

The transition was important to me because I needed to be true to myself. Living as a male was like living a lie. There never seemed to be any other solution for me, and I never meant to purposely hurt anyone.

Naive and unknowing of how people would perceive me, I expected everyone to be happy that I'd found my true self. I thought if I had confidence in myself and if I could demonstrate to others my sense of self-righteousness, people would rally around me. Sometimes I still feel this way, but I've learned to temper my enthusiasm. People are afraid of change. There's a fear of the unknown, and most people find comfort in staying on solid ground. I've learned that it's important to remain a little bit mysterious to others. Don't try to force yourself upon them. Let their curiosity find the good in you first. Later, as they come to know you better, when some mutual trust has developed, you can open up to them about more sensitive issues.

Gender transition is fraught with depression. Few people are able to avoid it. Imagine every heartfelt connection you have to others being disrupted, many of your family and friends failing to adapt to the change, and the loss becoming so great that sometimes you're not sure you can bear it any longer. Sadness and loneliness become part of your daily life. You yearn for acceptance, but you can't escape the guilt that consumes you.

Before I transitioned I felt guilty about my desire to change my sex, and after transition I felt guilty about the consequences of my decision. Children, spouses, parents, and friends—they all have to adjust, and the potential costs include divorce, financial loss, and alienation from the people you love.

Compartmentalization is common, and you find yourself trying not to remember the person you once were. Memories of your past, as much as you'd like to forget them, find their way into your consciousness, and you look for ways to rationalize their existence. You try to pretend they never occurred, but you know that's not true. You try to block them out of your mind, but they keep penetrating your defenses. Finally, after much soul-searching, you're able to tell yourself it's OK to have those thoughts; mental health professionals call this last step "integration."

Is transsexuality a mental illness or is it a biological phenomenon? I prefer to think it's the latter. I believe in the concept of brain sex, and I also believe it is not always congruent with the sex doctors assign at birth. Unfortunately, cultural expectations are at odds with this kind of thinking. Being a transsexual has its privileges, but it's also a curse. Experiencing life in both genders allows for a unique perspective of the universe but not without a price. At some point, almost every transsexual I know has felt forced to either confess his or her gender identity conflict or die, neither of which seems to be a good choice. According to a survey reported by the National Gay and Lesbian Task Force and the National Center for Transgender Equality, 41 percent of respondents reported attempting suicide compared to 1.6 percent of the general population.[1] Why is this the case? Why does our culture put such strict demands on our sexuality?

Reproductive development is like a professionally choreographed ballet. Everything needs to occur in sequence, at a specific time, with all the right players moving in precisely the right way, each displaying their craft

---

[1] INJUSTICE AT EVERY TURN: A REPORT OF THE NATIONAL TRANSGENDER DISCRIMINATION SURVEY; 2011; Lead authors in alphabetical order: Jaime M. Grant, Ph.D., Lisa A. Mottet, J.D., Justin Tanis, D. Min., with Jack Harrison, Jody L. Herman, Ph.D., and Mara Keisling.

with the proper amount of energy. When a mistake occurs, it changes the outcome of the dance.

Now consider the intersex individual, the one born with ambiguous genitalia, an extra X chromosome, or some other sex-linked biological defect. Scientifically, the male and female brains are known to be different, and the brain areas that are found to differ most between men and women are the ones in animal brains that have the highest number of sex hormone receptors during development. If the gonads develop in the first trimester and the brain in the third, how might an early developmental mistake affect the brain? Might a schism between the sex of the brain and that of the body occur? Is that any different from a birth defect that is visible?

I often hear people say, "I admire your courage to make the change that you did, knowing all the difficulties you must have faced." Strangely enough, I never felt courageous. Anxious and scared, trying to find a solution to a problem that at times seemed unsolvable was a more accurate appraisal. If there was any degree of courage, it came out of the fear of losing my sanity and the only good explanation for what I was feeling inside.

Oddly, once you've made the transition, the people you befriend will find it hard to imagine you as anyone but the person you now project to them. If only all the sadness and difficult memories of the past could be extracted to prevent their recall. Might that make the metamorphosis complete, or are those elements necessary for building character? If only I'd been born with a gender identity that matched my sex.

INFORMING ONE OF MY CLOSEST FRIENDS

I once had a good friend, Eleanor, who was a nurse and lived in Manchester. For years, she and I worked together, and we often confided in each other about our personal problems. Although Eleanor suffered from depression, she rarely looked sad to me. During a typical workday, she would tell me stories about herself or her family and then jokingly remark how crazy the world was. On that point, we never disagreed.

She was short with blond hair and had a clever smile. One day, with the permission of our spouses, we planned a day of kayaking and fishing on the Nashua River. I got up early and had coffee, got the boats ready, and bought bait at the local convenience store. Eleanor arrived at my house around eleven o'clock. She chatted briefly with Madge, and then we drove down to the boat launch.

There wasn't a cloud in the sky. It was a little hot, but there was a breeze on the river and no humidity. We put our hats on, lathered ourselves with suntan lotion, unloaded the boats into the water, and checked to make sure we had all of our gear. Eleanor had never kayaked on this river, so we spent the first hour or so just paddling upstream and enjoying the immensity of the scenery. The first thing we came across was a beaver swimming through some water lilies. He'd swim a little and then dive under the water only to pop back up again in some other spot a few minutes later. Just downstream from him, we saw a turtle sunning himself on a log. It was funny watching him stretch his head to catch bugs, but when we got too close, he dove for cover. If only we'd brought our cameras. What memorable photos we would have captured.

As we continued to paddle upstream, we reached what appeared to be a fisherman's monument. Someone had taken the bow of a boat and stood it upright in a cement base. We read the attached plaque that had a picture of a man and an epitaph etched into it, which related how much the man loved to fish this river. I thought it was a wonderful tribute to honor him in this way. I could only imagine what he must have been like. Maybe he'd had a son, and if he did, maybe he'd been a Boy Scout. I had been one during my youth, and although considered a masculine activity, it was a true joy for me. On Friday nights, we would gather at the Second Congregational Church and then hike five or six miles to get to the Scout camp.

It was a great place to go on weekends, and I have fond memories of catching fireflies, sitting around telling ghost stories at night, and trying to crank water from an old, rusted water pump. The stars always seemed to be out, and we would imagine ourselves as amateur astronomers, pointing out the difference between the Big and Little Dipper.

Frank Wilbur was our scoutmaster, and he loved watching over us. Our parents trusted him, and he never abused his privilege. He just liked having a lot of kids around. Most of the time, he was off fixing something, napping, or working in his shed. You could always ask him a question, but it was rare for him to know your name.

The camp had a central clearing with a dirt track surrounding it. Five or six cabins were scattered around the track, situated a short distance from the clearing. We were part of Troop 5. Inside our cabin we had a couple of gas stoves, a half dozen bunk beds, a separate bed for Frank, and a long picnic table where we would sit at night practicing our knots. To get a merit badge, I once had to start a fire in the middle of winter with only two matches. I cheated and had an extra book in my back pocket.

As I was reminiscing about those Scout days, a blue heron flew overhead. I looked over at Eleanor, and she had a dreamy-eyed look that told me she was probably reminiscing, too. The bird's nest was atop a large tree just off shore. What a wonderful sight it was.

As we headed back downstream, we found an inlet I had never explored before. It went into a narrow channel filled with cat o' nine tails and yellow water flowers. It was really pretty, and amongst the foliage we saw a couple of cardinals and some black birds with red breasts.

We then got out our fishing gear and looked for places to anchor our boats where the water was calm. All afternoon we drifted, until the slowly moving current pushed us into a log or a tree branch sticking out of the water, and then we cast our lines into the small pools and eddies that formed around them, hoping to find a secret spot where the fish had gathered. It was truly a memorable day.

A few months later, I called and asked if she would mind meeting me after work. I told her I had something important to share.

When she arrived, she inquired, "What's wrong? It sounded like you needed to speak to me right way!"

I didn't know where to start. What I was about to say would change her opinion of me forever.

"Eleanor, I've got to tell you something, something I have never been able to talk to you about before. I've…been seeing a psychologist."

As if granting me permission, she replied, "OK, so what's going on?"

I started to get this surreal sort of feeling. I could hear words coming out of my mouth, but it was hard to envision myself saying them. "I'm transgendered."

For a brief moment, she had a look of surprise, but then her facial expression changed to one that suggested an acknowledgement of how cruel the world could be.

"I would never have suspected," she remarked. A short silence occurred. "I think I should tell you something, too."

I thought to myself, "What secret could she possibly have that might be more incredible than mine?"

"You know those therapy sessions I go to? Well, the reason I get depressed is that Barney likes to cross-dress. I've thought about leaving him, but we keep trying to work things out. Are you telling me you're like him?"

Who could have ever imagined that her husband and I both had a gender disorder? What were the odds of that happening? To be honest, I just couldn't picture Barney dressed as a woman. He weighed close to 250 pounds, played on a softball team, and had a receding hairline. I tried to think of him wearing pink slippers and a woman's bathrobe, but I couldn't. Is this how people were going to think of me?

For a time, Eleanor and I were able to stay best of friends, and she remained accepting of me. We watched TV together, she shared her poetry with me, and she even offered to paint my nails. Nonetheless our relationship changed, and as time went on, I became so absorbed with what was happening to me that I forgot that important events occurred in her life, too. When she needed major surgery to remove her gallbladder, I dismissed it as something routine. Too wrapped up in my own problems, I failed to empathize with her. When she sent me an e-mail expressing some resentment, I wrote back suggesting she was upset with me because I was a reminder of what her husband might become. It was callous for me to say that, and even though I apologized and sent her flowers, our relationship never recovered.

ANOTHER FRIEND LEARNS MY TRUTH

My good friend John, whom I played golf with regularly, had a slightly different reaction. I called him one day and asked if he would mind coming over to my house. I told him that I had something I wanted to tell him. When he arrived, I met him in my back yard wearing a pink Red Sox shirt.

"What's going on?" he commented. "How come you're wearing that shirt?"

John and I had known each other for a few years. He was a patient of mine, and we had become friends because of a mutual interest in Apple computers and a fascination for the rapidly evolving Internet. It was a time when the technology was largely experimental. Most people didn't own a computer, and floppy discs were the only means of saving data. It was a time when you could only connect to the Internet by a telephone modem and the video on your screen was a frustrating display of choppy, black-and-white images. We chatted with AOL's instant messaging service and spent hours at a time exploring what might be possible with computers.

The boundary of our physician-patient relationship was often blurred, but I was young and had few friends outside of work. Computers were a passion of mine, and John loved tinkering with them, too.

When we weren't playing on the Internet, we were playing golf. It was a sport that allowed us time to be together, to philosophize about the world's problems, and to find out more about each other. We were pretty evenly matched, and the competition was always lighthearted and fun. For some people, golf is simply a game where you hit a small white ball (or a pink one) into a little hole, but it's much more than that. It can also be a metaphor for life. On any particular day, you might be able to partially master the complexity of the swing only to find that the next time you play, it totally eludes you. Golf, much like life, can be pretty complex at times, and it constantly requires you to reanalyze your successes and mistakes. For whatever reason, we both enjoyed it.

John was going to have to rethink everything he thought he knew about me. Madge and I took him by the arm and sat him down next to us at a picnic table in the backyard. I told him pretty much the same story I told Eleanor and then took a big breath of air.

He looked confused and asked, "How long have you felt this way?" and "What does the psychologist think about this?"

He tried to adjust.

In later months, he tried to play golf with me a couple of times, but I could sense he felt embarrassed in my presence, and our conversations quickly lost their gusto.

John surely struggled to find the answers to so many questions. Who is this person living inside my best friend's body? Where did the Jacob go that I once knew? Has he lost his mind? Did someone or something abduct him? I can't believe I've known him all of these years and yet never really knew him at all.

One day, after a long bike ride, I came home and started the water in the bathtub, grabbed a beer from the refrigerator, and settled in for a warm bath. It felt like heaven until I heard the doorbell ring. Adam hollered up to me, "Your friend is here."

I yelled back, "Let him in, Adam, and ask your mom if she'll make him a cup of coffee."

I climbed out of the tub and got dressed. As I walked down the stairs to the first floor, I heard Madge say, "He's on the back porch."

I went out to greet him and found him sitting on our wicker couch with the reading light shining on him, his silhouette an eerie contrast of dark and yellow.

"Hi, John. What brings you out tonight? Did Madge offer you something to drink?" I proceeded to sit in a chair across from him, still drinking my beer.

He disregarded my offer, and by the look on his face, I could tell this wasn't a pleasure visit. His feelings toward me were conflicted, and he wasn't sure he could remain my friend any longer. He remarked how, as the city electrical inspector, he was thinking of running for city office, and he didn't believe his association with me would bode well. Apparently, a few people who knew both of us questioned why I looked like *I was growing tits*.

I think he thought I might get sad and breakdown, but I didn't. I told him I understood how he felt and shook his hand. Before he left, I showed him how well I had wallpapered one of the bedrooms and then quietly said good night.

Madge questioned why I showed so little emotion, but I had no answer. It wasn't that I didn't hurt. It was just that I was in the process of a transformation. I was becoming a stranger to people who thought they knew me, and at times a stranger to myself as well. As Madge and I watched him drive away, I turned to her and said, "Maybe he will have second thoughts in a few weeks or a month. I don't know. It's best I don't let it bother me."

From then on, our friendship would never be the same. A year or two later, after I separated from Madge, he stopped by to see me one day. Although he seemed much the same to me, I could tell he saw me differently. He had trouble maintaining eye contact and paced across the room. He was searching for the friend he once knew, and he wanted to say goodbye. Finally, satisfied that he achieved his goal, he left and never called on me again.

FAMILY

Rockdale's department store was once an old mattress factory adjoining a canal in the town of Turners Falls, Massachusetts. When my dad was a kid, he and his friends would often float down the swift water of the canal on old mattresses they found near the factory. Sometimes they'd even climb atop metal bridges that spanned the canal and dive into the water. My dad always described his adventures as exciting, but in actuality, what he did seemed pretty dangerous to me, as the water below was very deep and there was no good place to exit the canal without help, at least not until you got closer to the Connecticut River.

When I was a boy, my dad would take my mom and me shopping at Rockdale's. Everything there was considered a bargain. Clothes were sold either on racks or in wooden bins, and the floor was made of hardwood planks that creaked when you walked on them. My dad loved going there because they sold popcorn, and we could eat it while we walked around. The factory windows were boarded up, and there was still a freight elevator to take you to the second floor. In addition to clothing, which was mainly stored on the first floor, there was a toy section and a tool section on the second floor. That's where I usually wanted to go.

Not too far from Rockdale's, there was a small neighborhood often referred to as the Patch. My dad grew up there, and during his childhood it was populated mainly by Polish and Irish immigrants. His friends called him "Maddie," and he once lived on the third floor of an old brick building next to a vacant lot. The Patch was not considered a wealthy part of town, but the people who lived there were proud of their heritage. Although my dad was of Irish descent, his sister married into a Polish family, and so I always felt I was part of both cultures.

Birthday parties and hotdogs, running downstairs to open presents on Christmas day, summer vacations at Hampton Beach, and shopping at Rockdale's were some of the happiest moments I spent with my family growing up. I wanted my children to have those kinds of memories, too. When they were young, I took them on bike rides, swam with them in our aboveground swimming pool, taught them to play Ping-Pong, and played countless hours of video games with them.

Telling my boys about my gender conflict often seems like one of the most selfish things I ever did, and I hurt them tremendously, but the confusion, the constant dialogue of thoughts playing out in my head, was an obsession, and the only way I could find relief from it was to talk about it. I've been told that it's important to be true to one's self, and most certainly I did not choose this condition—it chose me—but I often wish I had been strong enough to deny my feminine self and continue to live my life unchanged within the status-quo. Of course, in my mind, that would have been the same as death, but at least I wouldn't have traumatized my children. I was blind to the degree of sadness and grief I would cause them. Jonathan took it the worst.

For months I had contemplated ways of telling them my story, and one rainy day, after discussing my intent with Madge, I decided it was time. We ordered a pizza, and as we all sat down together at the kitchen table for our first slice, I began. I looked to Madge for guidance, and she gave me a slight nod of her head as if to say, "I wish you weren't convinced that you needed to do this, but if you've made up your mind, go ahead. I can't stop you."

I stared at Jonathan until I got his attention. He appeared to savor every bite of his pizza while remaining immersed in some daydream. Adam, who was sitting quietly next to him, seemed anxious for someone else to start talking.

As if unable to hold back the brake any longer, I blurted out, "Boys, I need to tell you something."

A hush came over the room, Adam looked at Jonathan for direction, and Jonathan, holding his pizza not far from his mouth, let the weight of it drag the end down.

I proceeded with my story. "I was born with a birth defect, and recently I started seeing a doctor about it. I know this is going to be hard for you, but I think I should have been born a girl."

There was no way they could have anticipated what I was about to say. They were caught completely off guard. It would have been better to tell them that I had a fatal disease than to tell them what I did, but I couldn't stop myself.

"For many years, I've had thoughts of wanting to be a woman. It's been driving me crazy and making me very depressed. I finally had to talk to someone about it. Your mom knows how much of a problem this has been for me over the years. I was born with a genital deformity that required surgery twice when I was younger. The doctor tells me it's possible that my brain was programmed to be female at birth, but because the rest of me developed like that of a male, I've been in a state of gender confusion since puberty. Can you understand what I'm trying to say?"

I must have appeared to be out of my mind. Could I really believe that after such a short discourse on gender theory, they would somehow miraculously understand what I had been trying to comprehend for years? How likely was it that they could possibly grasp a concept as complex as this, especially while in the middle of puberty and still struggling with their own sexual insecurities?

No, I knew they weren't going to handle it well, but I had to at least try to prepare them for the transformation. Like a caterpillar becoming a beautiful butterfly, my destiny was predetermined. The process was in motion, triggered by some genetic or environmental cue that I had no control over. To fight it, or try to slow it down, was futile. I knew there was not much time left, and I felt it was imperative to help them find a way to identify with the part of me that was alien, the part they had never seen before. It must have been overwhelming for them.

Not realizing that I might not be perceived as authentic, I tried to explain to them how I felt as a child, the humiliation I experienced when I failed to develop like the other boys, and how deeply I was affected by something I had no control over. They both looked at Madge, hoping she would give some hint that this wasn't true, just a cruel joke maybe, but her facial expression was one of confirmation and sadness. I continued to try to explain to them, in more detail, how I felt like a woman lived inside me, and I informed them that I was taking estrogen. They were speechless.

Suddenly Jonathan got up from the table and bolted out the front door into the rain. He took off running, and no matter how much I shouted his name, he would not stop or turn around and come back. Without any hesitation, Madge and I jumped into our van and drove to catch up with him. When he saw us coming, he started running faster, but eventually we were able to overcome him. When we knew that we had outdistanced him, we jumped out of our vehicle to both hug and apprehend him. Madge reached him first. He was crying, his teardrops indistinguishable from the drenching downpour. As he stood captive in Madge's arms, I didn't know how else to console him other than to put my arm around him as well. What had I done? How could I have been so callous, misguided, and hurtful? We coaxed him into the van and brought him home.

For months after this, both boys struggled to communicate with me. As time passed, the metamorphosis continued its stalwart progression. There was no denying it. I loved the creature developing within me. How could I not? But it was premature to expect others to have those same feelings. Instead, sadness, confusion, and rejection of the person I was becoming seemed to pervade their thoughts.

Of the two boys, Adam was more reserved, more forgiving than Jonathan, and he never stopped going to movies or playing video games with me. Sometimes I feel like I hurt him the most. I robbed him of his childhood innocence, and yet his response to my actions was always one of unconditional acceptance. If only he'd shown some anger toward me, pounded his fists on my chest, or screamed obscenities at me. Maybe then I wouldn't have had such feelings of self-reproach and sadness every night along with long periods of depression.

Over the next few years, Jonathan abandoned me for periods of time and asked me not to be part of his life. He said some horribly hurtful things to me, and worse, sometimes refused to talk to me at all. At times I felt I deserved his scorn, because I often put myself first and failed to recognize how my actions might affect those around me. I was reckless and self-indulgent, but it was part of a process that I seemed to have little control over. Was I mentally ill or just misunderstood? That is a question I can't answer.

The trauma I caused my parents is yet another story. One weekend, after inviting them to stay with us, I told them about my gender conflict in a less straightforward way. They had surmised for months that something was amiss, and they could tell that I was unhappy. Rather than say directly what was wrong, I handed them a copy of the suicide letter I had written for my doctor and stepped into an adjacent room. My mom read it silently as my dad peered over her shoulder. Then I heard my mother cry. That was my cue to reenter and try to explain it to them.

It was very difficult to tell them about my condition, and I was worried most about my dad, who had always been so supportive of me in the past. I was his first-born child, his oldest boy, and the "apple of his eye." Initially, he didn't know what to say, and it was obvious to me that he wasn't sure how he should react. Should he be hurt, angry, disgusted, or attempt to be sympathetic. He looked dismayed, and I knew it was best to avoid forcing a response from him. When he moved to another room, I chose not to follow him and instead tried to give him the time he needed to ponder his reaction.

He later told me that he thought it was just a phase I was going through, a sort of temporary insanity. Even after my gender reassignment surgery, he continued to have a hard time addressing me as "she," but true to his love for me, he never disowned me and eventually came to accept me for the person who I am.

As for my mom, she had a difficult time adjusting, too, and often expressed sadness with tears in her eyes, but her sadness didn't seem related to disappointment but rather to her own sense of guilt. She felt somehow responsible, as if it was her fault that I turned out the way I did. I always reassured her that I felt it was more likely a biological condition, but who knows for certain? Scientifically, there is much evidence to support a biological cause, but there are those in professional circles who still believe it's a product of nurture. All I know is that my mother kisses me now, buys me jewelry for Christmas, goes dress shopping with me, and helps me with my hair. Maybe she always wanted a girl, or maybe she feels bad about the way she treated me as a child. I'm not sure, but I do like her more at present than I ever did as a young boy.

As time went on, other family, friends, and coworkers made decisions about me as well, and their support, or lack of it, was generally unpredictable. I believe that how a person responds to gender diversity depends on how secure they are with themselves and their own sexuality. Many of those who responded negatively to me seemed to do so without really taking the time to get to know me. Many cited religious beliefs, but I find it hard to believe that a just and true god would not respect my desire to question creation and the dogma that surrounds our cultural beliefs. I believe the transformation allowed me to gravitate to a higher level of thinking. Without the experience, I would have remained an unknowing soul, one that lacked purpose, my mission on Earth an unfulfilled charge. Few would have the privilege to know what I was to learn about life in the months and years to come.

FINDING OUT MORE

A s the summer wore on, I became intensely interested in every aspect of gender. I read constantly on the subject. I scoured the Internet, my hospital library, and the local bookstores for anything that might pertain to it. No single article or book would satisfy my interest or my needs, but, instead, I found myself wanting to read ten more like it. Like a tree sprouting branches, I kept finding new areas to focus on.

I read autobiographies of transgendered individuals authored by Christine Jorgensen, Jenny Boylan, and Diana Rose. I found novels to read like *Trans-Sister Radio* that were humanistic attempts aimed at explaining gender identity. I read scientific papers on theories of sexual development, hormone discovery, brain sex, intersex conditions, and the controversy surrounding endocrine disruptive chemicals in the environment. I became fascinated with the history of important figures like Sigmund Freud, Havelock Ellis, Albert Moll, Magnus Hirschfeld, Harry Benjamin, and Margaret Sanger. I read about the nature versus nurture arguments proposed by John Money and Milton Diamond, the Kinsey Reports on human sexual behavior, Masters and Johnson's theories on human sexual response, and Ray Blanchard's theories of autogynephilia. I needed to have an explanation for why I was the way I was. Guilt was no longer a hindrance to my pursuit of knowledge, and I was determined to find the answers.

The more I read and the more I talked with Dr. Braunwald, the less inhibited I felt. I wanted to tell everyone what it was like to be transgendered. I wanted the world to experience the same satisfaction that I felt unlocking the door to the knowledge of sex and gender. What I failed to realize, though, was that not everyone wanted to know what was behind that door. My intense desire to inform others of what I had learned was not always welcomed. For many people, the subject matter was, and still is, taboo. Admittedly, I was often overzealous in my presentation. I published letters to the editor in the local newspaper, spoke at my local church, and campaigned at the New Hampshire state house for transgender rights while trying to change insurance company policies regarding hormone therapy for transsexuals. Although I was successful in making some people more aware of the transgender population, I was not always successful in swaying peoples' opinion favorably toward the transgender community or me, and in fact, I probably alienated some.

While my brain was changing, my habits and body were changing, too. I started biking every night and became obsessed with burning calories. I got my right ear pierced and wanted to pierce the left but figured it would be too much for people to accept all at once. Instead, I reasoned that once the right ear had healed, I could take the earring out and pierce the other side. Then when I was alone, I could wear the set.

By late summer of 2005, I became more daring with my wardrobe, and I started experimenting with wearing women's clothing that had an androgynous appeal to work. For example, a tight hooded sweater, a watch with minimal design but maroon narrow straps, or a thin black belt with a horseshoe-shaped buckle. I told my colleagues and patients that I was going through a mid-life crisis. In actuality, it was the truth.

How I saw myself in a mirror and the way I imagined myself to be were never the same. It was as if an alien lived inside me. My hands and arms had big veins from lifting televisions and washing machines at the appliance store where my dad worked when I was a teenager, and my shoulders were broad. I was tall for a girl, and I had some masculine facial features like a wide chin and a somewhat square jaw. My hair was gray, and I had a receding hairline, too.

In high school, I was a pole-vaulter on the track team. It was a passion for me, but vaulting, like lifting appliances, built up the muscles in my arms, too. I can't say that I have any regrets though, because for a couple of years, it was the highlight of my life. I loved the experience of vaulting myself into the air, and I was actually pretty good at it. At most meets, I typically placed first or second, and in my senior year, I even made it to the Western Massachusetts finals and placed fourth.

My rival was Morris. He lived just down the street from me, and we grew up together. We had become the best of friends. We even joined the track team together after a stint of cross-country running one fall. Morris was my equal as a pole-vaulter, and I daresay at times his strength and abilities were superior to mine. I enjoyed sports like track, gymnastics, cross-country, golf, and tennis because they were associated with both individual competition as well as group competition.

My passion for pole-vaulting came by chance, just as my passion for dance and ballet would come to me many years in the future, but what I wanted more than anything was to make my dad proud. I looked for him at every meet. He couldn't always be there because of work, but when I saw him on the sidelines, he was always an inspiration.

Sometimes it's hard to look back on that part of my life, because I don't always want people to know what I was like then. I was fiercely competitive, driven like a bull, and in deep denial of my feminine side. When I stared down that runway at the sunken metal box that I would jam my pole into, all I could think of was being the best. Speed and power and the image of my father reliving his childhood through me filled my thoughts. He wanted me to play on the track team at the University of Massachusetts after high school, and for a time it was my dream, too. We even sent away to California for a pole autographed by Bob Seagram, but after high school, I joined the Air Force and never vaulted again.

For a few years, I believed I could return to the sport in the future, but time marched on, and the only reminder I still have of those days is a picture of me vaulting in my high school yearbook. In medical school, I tore a ligament in my left knee playing basketball, dashing any dreams I still had of returning to my youth.

I've tried to make sense of all this and put my triumphs as a man in perspective with the transformation to my female self that occurred years later, but sometimes I can only do that by dissociating my new self from my old self, imagining the person I once was as simply an acquaintance. I know this sounds strange, but it's a defense mechanism that helps me maintain my sanity.

As I went through my twenties, thirties, and forties, it was easier for me to accept this fantasy rather than accept I was a transsexual. Looking back, I was always pushing the envelope. As time went on, I tried more and more to incorporate my cross-dressing behavior and feminine desires into the perception I had of myself. It wasn't long before androgyny just wasn't enough for me. I wanted to look pretty, to wear different style shoes, have hairless skin, and collect jewelry. I was determined to be someone different, but I didn't understand who that person might ultimately be until I started seeing Dr. Braunwald. She was a pivotal person in my life. She knew the kind of guilt and suffering I had been going through long before she ever met me. To her I must have been just another transsexual whom she had to try to prevent from self-destroying his or her life. She empathized with my condition, but she could see the inevitable crash that I couldn't see: the loss of friends and family, divorce, loss of employment, and financial loss. No matter what advice she offered, she was powerless to slow me down. How frustrating that must have been for her.

So what does all this say about me and others like me? A transsexual is an oddity of nature, with a destiny that may be predetermined. Like a monarch butterfly, a four-leaf clover, or an appaloosa horse, we are unique. It's not that we asked to be this way, it's simply what is, and learning to accept ourselves within the world we live is a major part of our transformation.

I could have bought a house with all of the money I spent transitioning. I gave up everything that once meant something to me, including the triumphs that once embodied my masculine self, to become a woman.

Coming out to the world at age forty-eight, I was a mixture of black and white, a rare gem amongst a sea of pebbles, someone whom at times favored life and at other times wished not to exist. It was a confusing time for me, and every day I still struggle with the ultimate question of "who am I?" The answer is always elusive.

My Day at
Bloomingdale's
Department Store

It was Thursday, September 22, 2005, and the weather was beautiful. It was sunny and cool with only a few clouds in the sky. I was on vacation and had scheduled an appointment at A & A laser in West Newton with Herly Pinto at 10 a.m. I was going there for a touchup on my arms, to remove unwanted hair. Herly was born in Brazil, and I had seen her many times in the past for similar treatments, but I had never told her I was a transsexual.

That day I was wearing a pretty brownish-red lady's sleeveless golf top with jeans, and I was carrying my red leather Etienne Aigner purse over my back like a knapsack. Herly didn't recognize me at first, but with a little prompting she remembered. She was happy to see me, but I could sense a little amazement in her eyes as she adjusted to the transformation.

Not quite sure what to say, Herly uttered, "I didn't know. It's OK though. I just didn't think—"

"That I was a transsexual?" I interjected. "I didn't know that I was either until just recently…when I started seeing a psychologist. Do you have a lot of people [like me] come here?"

"Yes, it's a good part of our business. You have two boys, don't you?"

"You remembered! I'm surprised. One is fourteen now, and the other is sixteen."

"How are they? Are they OK with you?"

"The younger one seems to be adjusting better than the older one. I've been told that's often the case. I just had to do this, you know. You don't think any less of me, do you?"

"Of course not, but I'm sure it must be hard for both of your boys."

I was glad we had the chance to be honest with each other. My appointment lasted about an hour, and we talked while she worked. She told me that her husband had recently lost his job. Herly's employer apparently didn't offer health insurance, and she was worried about the future and what would happen if anyone got sick. She felt her husband was depressed, and she commented that he seemed very quiet and withdrawn lately. I made some suggestions for getting her daughter fully immunized by using the State Health Department services, and I suggested a counselor for her husband. We ended the visit on an upbeat note, talking about the nice weather, and I told her I'd try to come see her again sometime.

It was my plan to stop at Bloomingdale's before heading home. I had discussed with Madge the possibility of doing some shopping in Boston that day, and she told me I could spend $100. That was my budget. I had been to Bloomingdale's only once, a few years earlier. At that time, I went there as my male self, only buying some socks and spending very little time looking at women's garments for fear of embarrassment.

There seemed to be a lot of affluent people in the store, and I saw women charging thousands of dollars and buying five or six dresses at a time. Many of them seemed to know certain sales personnel on a first-name basis. I heard one lady talking to her daughter in French.

It was strangely odd to walk around the store dressed as a woman and wearing make-up. For a transsexual, being able "to pass" is a highly prized achievement. I was feeling a little self-conscious, but I didn't notice any prolonged stares in my direction, so I felt I could relax. I was like a kid in a candy shop. What I lacked in confidence I made up for in a childlike innocence and desire to see myself in every outfit on display. I was having a grand time roaming from aisle to aisle and looking at things I'd never be able to afford when I saw it, what seemed to me an extraordinarily unique and beautiful sweater. It was made from wool dyed predominately olive green in a small checkered pattern with dots of pink. Little pink flowers were sewn delicately on the pockets and a pink ribbon to the right breast area. I fell in love with it, but it was a little more than $100, and I felt guilty that I'd be willing to spend that much on a sweater. The tag said "Sigrid Olsen, Antique Collection."

As I stood mustering the courage to buy it, a most wonderful saleslady saw me eyeing it and asked if I wanted to try it on. I tried to talk softly and with few words so she wouldn't detect any maleness in my voice.

"Could I?" I asked rather sheepishly.

"Of course, dear!" she replied as she walked me over to the women's dressing room.

Thus began a Cinderella-type adventure that lasted about an hour and a half and seemed an eternity. I had not expected such a joyous event to happen. The saleswoman had blond hair, looked to be in her mid-forties or early fifties, wore a purplish-blue suit, and spoke with a slight accent, British, I thought. She was pretty and a little taller than me.

She said, "Dear, let's try matching this sweater with a top."

She stepped away, and while I was admiring the fit of the sweater in the mirror, she returned with a couple more items for me to try on.

"What about one of these?"

I hesitated while trying to decide how to answer, and seeing that I was unsure, she said, "Wait I have a few more ideas. I'll be right back."

This pattern of coming and going with new articles of clothing continued, and she seemed to be having as much fun finding things for me to wear as I did trying them on.

At one point, she walked into the dressing room and saw me with my top off. I tried to cover my breasts but was only partially successful. If she knew I was a male, she didn't let on. Instead of looking away, she examined me from head to toe as if sizing me up.

"How about we try to find some pants that will go with this set?"

I replied, "I think I'm a size 14 but I've been trying 12's lately."

She left and brought back a pair of purple corduroys. "Here, try these. You know, you're definitely not a 12. I think you're an 8, dear. See how well these fit. You want them tight. They have elastic that stretches."

She was right, and I settled on three pieces: the sweater, a white top with a cool pocket on the sleeve, and a pair of cords to match. I told her I was on a budget, and although I loved all of the things she showed me, I couldn't possibly afford them all.

She said, "That's OK, dear, there's always next time."

When it came time to cash out, I stepped up to the register and realized I'd have to pay with my credit card. It was embossed with my real name, *Jacob E. Mathewson.*

"Maybe she'll think that's my husband's card," I thought, with a small degree of hope.

"Dear, I'll need to see your driver's license, too."

I handed it to her, knowing that if she hadn't figured it out already, she would know for certain now that I was a male. With my head slightly bent forward and with my best attempt at a soft voice, I said, "Do you get other people like me here?"

She looked at me as if none of that mattered. "Dear, you're beautiful. You don't need to worry about that."

What a nice thing for her to say. Even after the sale, she walked with me for a while and said things like "Isn't this nice? This would look good on you, too, you know."

For days and weeks afterward, I couldn't stop reliving that day. Memories like that helped sustain me and give me the character to face the turbulent times ahead. Human kindness is truly a wonderful thing.

TULIPS AND DANDELIONS

One night I was playing Mahjong, a Chinese tile game. The object of the game is to remove pairs of matching tiles from the board until there are none left. Sometimes you get stuck, and the tile you need is buried underneath another one. Sometimes, even when there are only a few tiles left, you can't see a match when there's still one present. Life can be like this; you can't always see the obvious until someone points it out to you.

On February 1, 2006, I appeared in court with a request to have my name changed. I had petitioned for the hearing some four or five months prior, and so I had been anxiously awaiting this day's arrival. I even sent invitations to all of my family and friends, and I included a wallet-size picture of myself with each one. I had a professional photographer take the picture, and I was wearing a cranberry-colored suit jacket with a cream-colored lace camisole. My hair was still short and parted slightly to the side with my bangs combed forward. I was wearing glasses with long hexagonal lenses and pretty frames. I wanted the photograph to reflect my new female self while also projecting a professional woman. I wanted the picture to show me happy, so I made sure to smile.

The invitations read:

> *Well it's official (and legal).*
> *As of 2/1/06, Jacob Everett Mathewson*
> *Is now*
> *Jessica Angelina Birch*
> *Please celebrate with me, in the*
> *Spirit of love and forgiveness,*
> *My transition to womanhood.*

My cousin and a few friends showed up for the hearing but not Madge, my parents, or my friends Eleanor and John. They all declined to come. They did not wish to be a part of this celebration.

Determined to make the day special, I wore a light-colored purple suit and had my picture taken with both my friends and with the judge who presided over the courtroom. He was an older man, but he seemed kind, and he was respectful of my request. He asked me a couple of questions but nothing out of the ordinary, and then he signed the document that confirmed my legal name change.

Here I must digress. While sitting in that courtroom, waiting for my turn with judge, I thought about all of the immigrants who had come to this country requesting citizenship. We shared a common bond; we both were celebrating a new beginning. Was the anxiety I felt about being there similar for them? Like many immigrants coming into this country for the first time, I was born to a working-class family. As they must've struggled with their social identity, so did I. I thought back to the time when I was a kid picking tobacco and working alongside migrant workers who spoke little English.

Throughout my life, I've generally resisted authority, maybe because I didn't grow up in a wealthy family or maybe because as a child I always felt like a "scraper," someone who believed you could never get what you wanted without a fight. My great-great-grandfather emigrated from Ireland, and he came to this country at the age of eighteen with a dream that he could become a success here. Maybe his drive to make something of himself was passed on to me.

During my transition, Dr. Braunwald often commented that I didn't respect boundaries. I was a physician, someone with a high degree of education. It was appropriate for me to address my patient's needs, but I was not supposed to be their friend. I continue to struggle with this issue. I have always had a difficult time separating myself from the downtrodden individuals of our society, and many of my patients are underprivileged. In some ways, I feel so much like them and identify with their needs.

Adding to my conflicting emotions, shortly after the hearing, Madge requested a separation. I knew it was coming. She told me one day that if I ever changed my name, she could no longer live with me. I made that choice without her permission and made arrangements to move in with Catherine Lonahue, a special person and a good-hearted soul, who had once been a patient of mine. I had been her physician about ten years earlier and lost track of her when I was transferred to another practice location. By a stroke of good fortune, she had taken a job as a medical records clerk and was assigned to work at my office. We reunited quickly and became good friends.

Catherine was born with a disability and lacked the lower half of her left arm. She was a little older than me and had never married, although she was once engaged. As a child, she was ridiculed, and as an adult, she often felt discriminated against. We both had difficulties obtaining acceptance from other people, and this became our common bond.

At first I was hesitant to leave Madge, but our relationship had become strained. I still loved her, but my transition had created problems for us that seemed insurmountable. When Madge's family had a special Mass for the one-year anniversary of her father's death, they asked me not to attend. I was hurt more than anyone could imagine. After all, her father's death played a crucial role in my coming out as a transsexual. Our parting was not without feelings of mutual regret, but at the time I was content to live life on my terms and to see where this adventure would take me.

My oldest son, Jonathan, and I were still struggling, too. One night he was alone at our house when I stopped by to check for mail. He was going through some old clothes of mine, and he looked sad. He had come across a Father's Day T-shirt that had the word "Dad" on the front, spelled in big letters. I was only planning to stay at the house for a few minutes, but seeing him in a state of depression worried me, and I felt I better not leave hastily. Up to that point, he had been reluctant to share his feelings about the transition with me. I asked him if there was anything I could do to make him feel better and if there were any questions I might answer.

He started crying and told me that he was angry with God over all that had happened. I hugged him and told him how I too had been angry with God for a period of time, until I came to the realization that there was no possible way anyone could truly understand the workings of God, let alone know for sure whether such an entity even existed.

I then said to Jonathan, "I am a dandelion in a field of tulips. For years, I've wanted to be a beautiful tulip. Now I realize that I'm just a pretty dandelion! If God can create the universe, the air, the trees, the grass, and all the living things in this world, why wouldn't he love a dandelion just as much as a tulip?"

You might ask where those words of wisdom came from and how did I come to this belief?

Dr. Braunwald and I often discussed spirituality. She helped me to think of the world in a different way. During one of my sessions, I remember her saying, "I believe that God is simply a projection of our own beliefs. Who's to say that a man can't wear a dress? It's just an article of clothing that keeps you warm. If you enjoy adorning yourself with jewelry and making yourself colorful by painting your nails and applying make-up, why should that be wrong?" I remember how profound these words seemed to me at the time. I cherished my time with her and confided all of my secrets and deepest convictions to her.

She challenged my whole sense of existence. The Catholic dogma of a heaven and a hell became no more a truth to me than that of a ghost story. Its intent to scare me and hold me hostage was no longer possible. Is sin anything more than our own conscience speaking? After all, who decides what a sin is? So what is our purpose on Earth? Is life simply a vehicle for learning some lesson, and then we die? What happens if we don't learn it? Do we have to come back and repeat life all over again? Could it be that we live many lives and learn something different from each one? Is there a grand scheme to life or do events just happen randomly without reason? How queer my mind works sometimes.

Jonathan and I continued our discussion for a while longer. I talked to him about the prejudice and injustices of the world. I told him how I had a new appreciation for what it felt like to be a minority. I was hoping I might reach the half of his brain that had received its genetic code from me, the part of him that questioned his own reason for existence. His mother was content to accept the world for what it was, and although she could be a friend to just about anyone, she was strict in her beliefs and never wavered. I didn't want him to listen to that half of himself that night.

I left him to go watch my other son, Adam, play basketball at the local junior high school, and when I called the house after the game was over, his mood seemed much more uplifted and peaceful.

The next night, I stopped at the house again to see how he was feeling. I knocked on the door, and after a brief wait, the door opened with both of my boys standing there to greet me. Jonathan looked more relaxed and he seemed to be in a better place. He had been watching television with Adam. The sadness I had seen the night before was no longer visible.

"Is it OK if I come in?" I asked.

Madge was stretched out on the couch. She turned and twisted her head to look over at me as the boys stepped back to allow my entrance. In an apparent gesture to avoid confrontation, she asked with some hesitation, "How are you?"

"OK, I guess. Can I come in?"

No one voiced any objection, although I sensed some ambivalence. To ease the tension, I started a conversation by asking them all what they were watching on television. I wanted to belong here again, to be part of the family. Soon we were talking about school, the latest downloads on iTunes, and how well Adam had been playing basketball in his youth league. Madge remained quiet and reserved although respectful.

Jonathan had been taking guitar lessons for a few years, and I suggested he play something for us. His guitar, not far from his reach, was one I had bought for him one Christmas. He started to play, and we were all mesmerized by his skill. My own guitar, an Alvarez, was still at the house and upstairs in the spare room. Jonathan knew it was one of my prized possessions. I told him that if he was careful, he could go get it and play it for us. His eyes gleamed, and he ran upstairs to retrieve it. He came back down and placed it across his lap. A big smile came to his face as he began to make the strings resonate. You could tell he loved the sound it made. In his hands, the instrument took on a lovely animated look, respectful of his expertise and willing to give its all for him. It was beautiful to watch. Myself, I was only a mediocre guitar player and hadn't practiced in years. I would never learn to play as well as he did.

Reminiscing back to a time when I first started taking lessons, I asked him to learn a couple of songs for me: "Mr. Bojangles" as sung by David Bromberg and "Circle Game" sung by Joni Mitchell. He was thrilled, and he started right away looking on the Internet for sheet music with the cords and notes. While researching the "Circle Game," he gleamed when he noted that to play it correctly, you had to retune the guitar so that the fifth and sixth strings were both E strings, and you needed a capo positioned on the second fret. I had forgotten that.

Later that evening, trying again to act like a family, we played the game Upwards, and then we watched a movie together. When it was time for bed, Jonathan said, "I love you, Dad." I asked Madge if it was OK for me to stay the night, and she agreed. I slept in the spare room, and it felt good to be back in a familiar bed. The next morning, I went back to Catherine's.

MOVING FORWARD

Being true to oneself is not always without suffering. The excitement of the coming months was tempered by mistakes in judgment, and I was unaware of the deep-seated prejudices ingrained in even the most open-minded of individuals. There was no turning back, however. I could think of nothing else but how to achieve my goal. I wanted to explore every aspect of being female.

My days soon revolved around hours and hours of electrolysis, therapy visits, laser treatments, voice lessons, and an occasional doctor's appointment. Whereas I could barely talk to girls in grade school, now I could be part of their world without any sexual undertones. If I wanted to sew, play with make-up, shop for clothes, browse boutiques, or go to dance class, I was no longer prohibited. There was so much new to discover.

Pam Nottingham was an electrologist. Her office was just down the street from mine. I had passed it many times over the course of a few years without realizing its existence. One day I noticed the sign in front of her building. It read: Face Works, Electrolysis by Pam Nottingham.

That evening, after work, I decided to visit her and inquire about an appointment. She was located in a long white building that included a karate studio and a carpet cleaning company. As I walked into the building, her office was to my left and blocked by a heavy wooden door.

"Maybe she's closed," I thought.

When I turned the knob and gave the door a shove, it opened into a small, brightly lit waiting area with a couch and one chair, a coffee table, and a candy dish atop it. There was a glass partition on the far wall, and in another room beyond the glass, there was some office equipment but no receptionist. There was not a soul in either room. Did someone forget to lock the door?

"Maybe I shouldn't be here," I said to myself.

In the distance, in some other room, I could hear two women talking and exchanging good-byes. Suddenly I heard a voice, and the door off to the side of the waiting room opened.

"Can I help you?" said a rather beautiful woman with shoulder-length brown hair wearing a long white lab coat.

I wasn't sure what to say. I wanted an appointment, but I didn't know how to ask for one.

"Are you the electrologist? I've never been in an office like this before. Do you mind if I ask how much electrolysis costs?" Then I paused before blurting out, "Does it hurt?"

"Well, I'm actually just getting ready to close, but what part of the body were you thinking of having me work on? My usual rate is $60 an hour or $40 for a half hour. It hurts a little bit, but a lot of people put a topical anesthetic on before they get here. That seems to help. Do you want to come back another night?"

I was still quite masculine in appearance. If I asked her to work on my face, would she think I was queer? I wasn't gay, and I didn't want her to have that impression of me. I wasn't changing my appearance to be more attractive to a man. I was changing my appearance because I loved the role of being female. That's an important distinction for transgendered people. Gender identity, gender role, and sexual preference are all separate components of what makes up the sexual being within each of us. For most people, those three entities are congruent, but in transgendered individuals, that's not the case. Furthermore, sexual preference in transsexuals can change.

When I met Pam, I still had my male body, and I felt an attraction to her. She was pretty, and she had a nice smile. I wanted her to feel that we had a heterosexual connection, but similarly, I didn't want to alienate her or make her feel uncomfortable, as I really needed her services.

I decided it would be best to be up front with her. "I'm transgendered. I was wondering if you could work on my face?"

She took a moment to rethink her mental picture of me. "Sure, I could do that."

"How many visits will it take? Is it a long process?" I asked.

As if hesitant to answer my question truthfully, she said, "Well, it can sometimes take many hours and many visits to achieve a good result."

Little did I realize that I was soon to start a process that would require some four hundred hours of treatment at a cost of nearly twenty thousand dollars before I would be satisfied with the result. Of course, this was spread out over a few years time. On each occasion that I met with Pam, I found new ways to deceive myself into believing that I only needed a couple of more sessions. Like a compulsive gambler, I kept thinking the payoff was just one hand away.

"So you wouldn't mind working on me?"

"I'd be happy to. Do you want to come back next Thursday at seven o'clock?"

Thus began the start of our friendship and a new chapter in my life. My visits with Pam soon became routine, and electrolysis became as familiar to me as having lunch at the local diner, stopping for gas, or buying a coffee.

Sometimes I would go for two or three sessions in one day, each lasting anywhere from one to two hours. The assault on my nervous system seemed never ending. Even with the use of a topical anesthetic, two hours was about the maximum I could tolerate at any one time. After the first hour or so, every fourth or fifth insertion of the needle would cause my chest to heave and my right leg to jump uncontrollably, as if the electrical energy had reached a pivotal threshold and could no longer be contained. Trying to inhibit the process was impossible and only served to make the contractions more powerful.

In an effort to comfort me, Pam would play music from her CD player and talk with me. She was as much my therapist as Dr. Braunwald. I would tell her about my childhood, the struggles I was going through in my personal life, and my difficulties at work. In turn, I got to know what kind of music she liked, what her interests were, what foods she enjoyed, and the precarious relationship she had with her boyfriend.

"He's so cheap you know. He never wants to spend money on anything. Last weekend he took me out to this really nice restaurant, and the whole time we were there all he did was complain about the cost of the meal. Four years we've been dating, and he still hasn't bought me a ring."

While lying on the exam table, trying to absorb everything Pam expounded, an unspoken trust developed between us. We needed each other. To say I wasn't attracted to her in the beginning would be a lie, but over time our relationship changed. As I became more female and the sexual drive of my male psyche lessened, Pam was able to find in me a friend who knew the workings of the male mind and yet was committed to aligning with her female side. Although she often seemed to fail in her relationships with men, she was a presence among other women, and they all looked up to her. I wanted to know what she knew about women and how they interacted with each other, so I made an effort to help her understand her boyfriend's motivations, and she helped me understand the bonds of sisterhood.

One of the many things we had in common was a love for animals. Pam had a Portuguese water dog named Nina who went everywhere with her. One of the first things we did together, that was not client related, was to go for a walk with Nina after one of my appointments. I remember how awkward it seemed at first, neither of us quite knowing our role, but one thing led to another, and soon we found ourselves comfortable in each other's presence. We shopped together, we experimented with new foods at delicatessens and health food stores, and we took rides to Portsmouth and the beach. Once we even spent a weekend on a farm in Maine with one of Pam's childhood friends. The three of us baked a blueberry pie and later drove into Augusta to party at a nightclub where we let drunken men buy us cocktails and ask us if we'd like to dance. Thankfully, it was somewhat dark in there.

One day, while I was lying on the exam table and she was working on me, I opened up to her about my birth deformity, how I endured the taunts of playmates, and the physical abuse of my mother. The pain of the electrolysis needle seemed nothing compared to the emotional pain I had kept inside for so many years. Although she wore surgical gloves, her hand resting on my face was comforting. I could feel a tear running down the side of my cheek, but I didn't try to wipe it away. I didn't want to hide it from her; I wanted her to see my vulnerability. I was lying on my side, in a purposeful way, facing away from her, unable to look directly at her. I didn't want her to see my eyes, lest they give away all the secrets and ugliness of my past. I just wanted her to listen, to be my witness, and to help me justify my actions to others. I needed to forgive all those who had harmed me in any way, and I needed her help to forgive myself.

She continued with her treatments, slowly and methodically applying electricity to each hair follicle on my cheek and then plucking it from its root. She remained silent, for the most part, as if sharing my pain and misfortunes and trying to relate them to her own.

It was risky telling Pam my innermost secrets, but I felt I could trust her. We had grown fond of each other's company, and I felt it unlikely that she would betray the trust between us. She never made me feel like I was any less of a person for what I was doing, and whenever I felt that big void deep inside, it was comforting to know I could talk with her.

Not wanting her to pity me, and realizing that I'd spent enough time telling her about my past, I decided to come back to the present and focus my attention on her.

"Well, that's enough of that talk," I said. "What do you say after we finish up here we go get some lunch?" The music of Zero 7 was playing in the background, Nina was getting anxious to go outside, and our session was almost over.

"That sounds good. What about driving over to the Lobster Boat? I think they have a lunch special today." Pam acted as if nothing unusual had happened between us. I had entrusted to her a part of my soul, a most vulnerable part that had been injured many times in the past, and she accepted it for safekeeping.

As time went on, Pam and I remained close. Without her, I would have missed an important part of my development. I have so many good memories of the times we spent together during the early years of my transition. We made adventures out of everything we did, from shopping for shoes to buying clothes at Macy's department store. Cooking dinner was always a treat, and we could spend hours browsing boutique shops looking at greeting cards, soaps, accessories, and jewelry. She taught me the difference between warm and cool colors, and she cautioned me never to wear orange. She helped me learn how to apply make-up, and using her electrolysis skills, she shaped my eyebrows. With my permission, she even tattooed permanent eyeliner to my eyelids in a beautiful shade of blue.

In turn, I tried to be there for her when her stepfather and her father died, when her boyfriend left her, and when Nina had to be put to sleep after developing rectal cancer and exhausting Pam's financial ability to care for her.

Like the sea, constantly moving, shifting, responding to the moon's gravitational pull, the ebb and flow of life is in a constant state of flux. We are molded by a force more powerful than any man or beast can possibly comprehend. Emotional wounds can heal very slowly sometimes. Having someone to confide in, someone willing to accept you for yourself along with all of your faults can be a powerful source of healing.

TRYING TO FIND MY WAY

Madge and the kids had gone away for the weekend. Although I no longer lived at home, Madge asked if I would mind stopping by the house to check on Skip, our family dog. He was a toy fox terrier that we once bought for the kids as a pup, giving him to them one Christmas as an unexpected gift. He weighed about twelve pounds, was white with black spots, and had a somewhat protective disposition. I always loved animals and found Skip to be great company, so when Madge asked me if I'd watch him for her, it really wasn't a chore at all.

As I pulled into the driveway, I noticed that the neighborhood was pretty quiet, and I couldn't help but wonder if someone wasn't peeking out of their window to get a glimpse of me. After all, I hadn't lived there for over six months, and everyone knew why I moved away.

I opened the door to my car and stepped out quietly, wearing a green dress and double strap short black heels. I stood for a moment and surveyed my surroundings. I could now dress however I wanted and had no fear of condemnation. In times past, when Madge would go away for a weekend, I would wait until late at night, when it was dark outside, and then I'd sneak into the back yard wearing woman's clothing and make-up. I'd sit at a table on the patio and imagine that it was daytime, that I was having tea with a girlfriend, or just taking in the noonday sun. I was acutely aware of sound, and if I heard the slightest noise, I would rush back in the house or hide behind the shed. Sometimes I'd get really brave, open the gate to my backyard, and make a dash to my car. I'd hover in a crouched position, checking to make sure no one saw me, and then quietly get in the car and take it for a drive around the block.

How different my life had become in one year's time. All that prowling around now seemed absurd. As I entered through the front door, Skip barked briefly but then started wagging his tail as soon as he recognized me. I took a seat on the couch, gave a thought to my eventual mortality, and then took some time to contemplate my life.

I was thirsty, but I had no desire to eat. The antidepressant that Dr. Gransby had prescribed a few days before made me feel oddly out of sorts. I had agreed to take it at her request, although I was shocked initially when she made the suggestion. Was I one of those patients, someone emotionally unbalanced who needed to take a pill to maintain her sanity?

I looked around the room and admired the moldings that surrounded and defined the ceiling. One summer, I had painstakingly used a coping saw to join all the corners, scalloping the wood to conceal the seams. It was quiet and somewhat eerie as I roamed about the house. As I looked around, all I could see was the sadness of unfulfilled dreams. The walls in the hallway that I had always wanted to paper were still the rose color I had painted them over fifteen years ago, and they looked neglected. A dent in the sheetrock along a wall heading up the stairs was still there and in need of repair. I had planned to fix it before procrastination set in and I lost my desire.

The two-person tub in the bathroom that was an addition to the original floor plan looked unused, except as a receptacle for plants that needed water. I loved that tub. I spent weeks discussing its construction with the builder. A few years after we moved in, lacking a way to visualize the outside world while taking a bath, I had a carpenter build a window for me in the shape of a hexagon. I spent many a night after work soaking in that tub, sometimes for hours. In the winter, I'd fill it with hot water, and it would be my refuge from the cold.

I wandered into the bedrooms. Nothing was put in its proper place. The beds were unmade, furniture appeared dusty, and articles of clothing were strewn on the floor in the master bedroom amidst pieces of old wrapping paper. There was laundry that needed to be put away and pillows that lay lifeless on the floor.

Adam's room seemed the same. Numerous posters and calendars of the Red Sox, along with portraits of sports figures, were still tacked to the walls just as I remembered them.

The room I often claimed as mine was now Jonathan's. My computer was gone, and all vestiges of things that were once mine had been removed. The beautiful curtains I had bought, patterned with pretty red flowers, were gone. The walls, once a pleasant pastel green with an attractive border, had been sponged blue and the border removed.

The alarm system was no longer being monitored, but it was still in place. Small white detectors present in the hallway and the kitchen were lifeless now. Little red lights that once signaled their presence were no longer lit.

There was a stillness in the air. The house had aged without me, and it had become a monument to what could have been.

The once beautiful white wooden fence that surrounded the backyard was now dull and dirty. It was in need of repair and a fresh coat of paint. The trestle that once prefaced the front gate and the beautiful trumpet vine that I trained to weave through the slats had been removed, leaving the entrance bare. The pretty tulips, irises, and black-eyed Susans I once planted were now gone.

The backyard had large areas of dirt without grass. My blueberry and raspberry bushes were gone, and nothing had been planted in their place. Why would anyone do this? Where were the bleeding hearts? Alas, they had been cut down, too, I'm afraid, to leave no degree of emotion remaining in this place.

In the summer of 1993, I planted an ornamental cherry tree, a locust tree, birch trees, a rose bush, and flowering forsythia. To ensure their success, I dug huge holes, removed rocks, and filled the holes with soft soil, fertilizer, and peat moss. The soil came from a large mound of loam left by the builder at the end of our street. I would cart the dirt to my house using a wheel barrel, pushing it about the length of a football field. It was a summer of hard work, and I often toiled late. By the end of the evening, dirt and sweat covered my body, and my muscles ached so much that I found it difficult to fall asleep. But it was my love of art and the beauty of nature that sustained me. I was determined to create a masterpiece.

I had such grand plans for this home. Now none of it mattered. The bushes and the trees I planted were still there but seemed lifeless. I wanted to hug them, especially the trees, because I loved them most. I wanted to say that I was sorry for abandoning them. If they could speak, would they also resent me for leaving them? Would they, too, hate me?

I walked back into the house, sat again on the edge of the couch, and stared into space. Time seemed an everlasting commodity. Every breath seemed measured, and I didn't want to move or leave the spot I was in. I wanted something I couldn't see or touch, something that was difficult to define. I longed for a life that would never truly be mine, and my own accomplishments seemed minuscule in comparison to others.

I decided to take a nap and found myself in a dream. I was with a woman, and she was asking me if I wanted to go to lunch with her. She was smiling, and we were standing outside in the sunshine. I wasn't sure at first if I knew her, because I couldn't make out her face, but then it slowly came into focus, and I realized it was my friend Meredith. We were standing on a street corner, as if waiting for something.

Abruptly the scene changed, and I found myself driving my car with her in the passenger seat. Oddly, I knew I was in a dream, because when I closed my eyes, I could still see the street. As dreams often go, I found myself outside of the car but unable to speak. I thought about calling someone on the phone, but how would I converse with that person? I tried to write something, but my arm wouldn't move. I struggled to open my eyes, but I couldn't. Finally, using all of my powers of concentration, I was able to wake up, but it wasn't easy, and I awoke scared and wondering what would have happened had I stayed in that *locked in* state.

Later, I thought about that dream and how it related to my life. Something inside me was changing. A powerful force was at work, and I could no more prevent it from affecting me than I could understand its ultimate objective. In some strange way, I knew my survival depended on letting the process go to completion, but how could I explain this to anyone else when I didn't understand it myself.

Then a thought came to mind. Was I missing the obvious again? Was the estrogen I was taking causing changes to occur in my brain that were affecting my thought processes? Is that why I felt so strange? Was I in control or was I simply responding to a chemical messenger that nature devised to preserve the species? I pondered the answers for a moment.

I had become so focused on my gender dysphoria as the cause of my emotional instability that I forgot to consider the fact that maybe the estrogen I was taking was in part responsible for my emotionality. Of course, the gender dysphoria preceded my taking estrogen, but was I becoming an addict to the effect of the latter? Was I going to become attracted to guys or wish I could have a baby?

I had inadvertently devised an experiment to test the effects of cross-sex hormone treatment on humans and had become both the scientist and the test subject. Relating my experience was to become a matter of necessity. Estrogen and testosterone differ by only four atoms of hydrogen and one of carbon, yet their effects on our appearance and personalities are drastically different. I was determined to understand how this was possible.

Male and female brains are different both in structure and the way they process information. Neurocognitive function is extremely complex and, for the most part, still poorly understood. What is known is that the brain has an abundance of sex hormone receptors that bind with androgens and estrogens produced by the gonads. These chemical messengers are thought to play a role in both brain development as well as function. For example, women tend to use more intonation in their speech and choose from a larger vocabulary of words than their male counterparts. Although a woman's brain is generally smaller than a man's, women possess a greater density of neurons in the temporal lobes, which may explain why they are better at coloring their speech. Whereas a man might say, "It's a nice day," a woman might express the same opinion by saying, "Isn't the weather wonderful? What a beautiful day it's going to be."

Another area of the brain, called the hippocampus, is associated with memory storage and spatial mapping of the environment. This part of the brain is located within the limbic system located in the medial part of the temporal lobe. It too appears to function differently in men and women. Whereas a man is likely to navigate by estimating distance, women tend to navigate by landmarks.

Lastly, the amygdala, again located in the limbic system, appears to be associated with the memory of emotionality. Using specialized brain imaging (PET scanning) combined with visual stimuli, researchers have learned that this part of the brain processes information differently in men and women; it is typically more active on the right side in men and more active on the left in women.

Are any of us really in control of our actions and motivations? I think sometimes we fear the answer to that question. An internal electrical pacemaker governs the rhythm of our heart, the billows effect of our lungs is driven by the contraction of our diaphragm, and our muscles are nothing more than pulleys. We are, in a sense, machinelike. Do we have a purpose or do we just exist? It's no wonder so many people suffer from depression, alcohol and drug abuse, and other mental health disabilities.

The weekend ended rather uneventfully, and I returned to my daily routine of worrying about the future, trying to justify my existence, and making sense of all the craziness in my head. I continued to see Dr. Braunwald about every two weeks. It was a very emotional time for me, and never having had a therapist before, I opened up to her about everything, including some things in my past that I'd never told anyone before. I needed to get it all out, to spill my guts so to speak. I was a tormented soul, and my subconscious mind was trying to process and integrate a new sense of self-awareness.

At night I would take long bike rides, always following the same route and pedaling as fast as I possibly could. I became obsessed with reminiscing about my childhood, the military, my family, and all of the events that were unfolding for me at work. It wasn't healthy. An abyss of regret consumed me. When I felt this way, I would often think about Dr. Gransby. Her life fascinated me. She and her husband skied whenever they had the chance, climbed mountains, and were always traveling to some exotic place. She seemed so determined to live life to the fullest.

Me? I was in a rut. I longed for adventure and lusted for a deeper appreciation of the arts. I often imagined Dr. Gransby as my childhood friend, and I missed never having had the opportunity to know her when we were both young. I once made her a three-dimensional collage of two young girls sharing fun times together and gave it to her at an office appointment. I explained to her that in making it, I imagined it to be symbolic of us as children doing things best friends do together.

She grinned and took it in stride. "I must be the blond one," she said.

As time went on, we remained good friends. I e-mailed her frequently, and she was always gracious in her replies. I envied her so much. "If only I could be like her," I thought.

DR. GRANSBY

DID I KILL JAKE?

Is Jake dead? I didn't mean to kill him! Maybe he's just sleeping. Yes, my name is Jessica Angelina Birch.

It was Saturday. My brother had invited Madge and the boys, my parents, and my aunt and uncle to his house. They had left a few hours earlier, but I wasn't invited. He told Madge that he didn't want his kids to see me because it would be too confusing for them and they wouldn't understand my appearance. Unable to have children themselves, they had adopted two infants from Ethiopia. They were still young: a girl three years old and a boy five.

As I pondered what to do, I said to myself, "Why couldn't my brother call me himself and tell me that I wasn't invited? Why should I care if he doesn't want me at his house? Would his kids really care? They'd likely be more interested in playing with their toys than staring at me. Anyway, what would I do once I was there? Try to explain for the hundredth time why I wanted a different life! Why is it so hard for them to understand! What's so wrong with me anyway?"

It had been an emotional week. I had opened up to Dr. Braunwald and told her shameful things about myself, like how I stole women's garments as a child and wore them under my clothes to school. I couldn't afford to pay for them, and even if I could, I never would have been able to look the salesperson in the eye. I had to choose between being unlawful or immoral, and both were considered scandalous. I hated being a boy. If only I had been born a girl—*sigh*—my parents would have bought them for me. I would have been able to choose the color and the style, and the people shopping with me would only have been concerned about how the garments were constructed or what fabrics they were made of.

Dr. Braunwald didn't seem concerned about the stealing. She said, "That was a long time ago. You were fighting something you didn't understand. You don't need to feel guilty about it anymore." I wept and felt my heart sink. I was feeling like I was both the defendant and the jury at my own trial, and nothing made sense to me anymore. It strained my intellectual being. My thoughts were like bursts of energy and light, traveling erratically, colliding into each other while trying to find their way to their ultimate destination in my brain. How would I know if I was sane? Maybe I wasn't! Could I have a brain tumor? Maybe this was all a dream.

I made arrangements to have breakfast with my friend Julia at her jewelry shop. Whenever I was troubled in the past, she often had answers for me. I brought bagels and cream cheese for us, she made coffee, and while I watched her work, we talked. I was wearing my jeans with the embroidered flower patches, the thumb ring that she had made me, and my Annie Hall hat. A few days earlier, my hairdresser had dyed my hair reddish auburn, and I wore my new pearl earrings that my roommate Catherine had given me.

Julia sensed I was troubled. As we were toasting the bagels, she said, "Something's bothering you. Do we need to talk about it?" I told her I was still feeling guilty about my past, and she asked, "What do you feel guilty about?" I hesitated and answered, "Stealing!" She responded, "You mean stealing clothes. You already told me about that. Is there anything else?"

"I'm not sure who I am anymore." I told her I was worried that I was losing my mind and that I didn't seem to have control of my life anymore. A few months earlier, in December of 2005, my employer had placed me on paid medical leave. The administrators of the company had become uneasy with all the physical changes that were occurring in me and were worried about the effects on my patients. I told Julia I wasn't sure that I was prepared for a full day of psychological testing two weeks from now with Dr. Jukowsi. With my permission, my employer had arranged the appointment in an effort to determine if I was capable of returning to work. Who was I becoming? What was happening to me? How do you explain to others that you believe you have two people living inside your head, each with a distinct personality, different from each other but not separate? Only another transgendered person could possibly understand the confusion, the internal struggle, I was experiencing, as I tried desperately to define my true self.

Julia looked at me and asked, "Does Jessica Birch want to be a doctor?"

I had to think for a minute, "I believe she does!"

I further tried to make light of the situation by suggesting that I'd like to be a fashion designer, but Julia interjected, "You need to be sure, because that's what your employer wants to know. I liked Jacob. He was a good doctor. He was compassionate. He liked to talk about science, his dog, and kayaking with me. I have many girlfriends, but Jacob was one of the few male friends I've had that I felt I could trust, and you killed him. You didn't give anyone time to say good-bye to him."

The verdict was in. Guilty! She was right. In my haste to become Jessica, I hadn't given people time to grieve for the loss of Jacob. To my family and friends, it was if I had hijacked him, tied him up, and hid him away in some remote part of my brain so no one else could find him. I never meant to harm anyone. I just wanted a chance to live.

Not that long ago, when I first started to see Dr. Braunwald and shortly after my forty-eighth birthday, I learned that according to the American Psychiatric Association I was considered to have a "gender identity disorder," a type of mental illness. I also learned that knowledgeable mental health professionals, those who have experience caring for transgendered patients, generally don't feel it's a mental health disorder at all but rather a normal variation of human sexuality. In either case, my life had become a mess. I couldn't tell if I was sick or just misunderstood? Old friends now shunned me, family members no longer seemed at ease with me, my own son requested that I not attend his sixth-grade graduation, and my employer was contemplating my dismissal.

Jennifer Boylan, a noted transsexual and an English professor at Colby College, once wrote in a letter to me, "Gender identity disorder is probably the only medical condition that gets better, as it causes increased suffering to those the patient cares most dearly for." This was becoming my experience, too!

Julia sensed I was feeling remorse and added, "You need to let parts of Jacob still express himself. He can help you. You can't just forget him and discard him like an old suit."

As I left to go home, Julia gave me a big hug and told me she would be working late Sunday night, and she suggested I come see her again before my meeting with the psychologist. As we parted, I said, "Jessica's a good person, too!"

She replied, "Did I say she wasn't?"

A few days later, I stopped by the house to visit with my boys and found Madge sitting at the end of her bed getting dressed. She had her back to me, and she was pulling up her slacks. I stared in her direction, my conversation with Julia still fresh in my mind. Madge looked like someone who had recently lost her best friend. There was a sadness that I couldn't console. Neither of us really wanted to hurt the other, but we couldn't seem to find a means of compromise. I couldn't live as Jacob anymore, and she didn't want to be married to a woman.

As she turned in my direction, I asked, "Did I kill Jake?"

She paused, contemplating her response. During the early stages of my transition, she had done what any loving wife would do: she tried to understand her husband's illness and be supportive. But as time progressed, and the illness took the course it so often does, she found herself helpless as she watched the man she married transform into a being she no longer knew. Each day it seemed as if another piece of him was gone. What was this thing taking her husband from her? She had tried talking to a counselor, but her Catholic upbringing was too strong, and she could not allow herself to be in a lesbian relationship. As Jacob slowly faded away, her grief over his loss became mixed with anger as she learned more about Jessica. She hated Jessica. In her mind, she was a thief, and it wasn't until Jacob was no longer recognizable that she felt it safe to say so.

Madge turned her head slowly in my direction. With eyes wide, and a bitterness perceivable in her facial expressions, she stared at me as if I was an invader from another world. "I don't know you anymore. I can't live with you as a woman."

In her mind, the man she married had died. He had committed adultery with himself and then allowed the adulteress to take his life. What was happening to us was beyond the average person's comprehension. Madge could not accept being married to a woman. It was not in her nature. For a few years, we both sensed our lives were going in different directions. We both knew our marriage was in trouble, but neither of us was willing to openly speak about it to the other. We tried desperately to deny what was happening to us. We we're hoping to find a solution, but we had finally come to the realization that the search was over and there was no place left to look.

"If I had given you more time to adjust, would you still want a divorce?"

She replied, "We haven't been honest with each other for a few years now. I should have done something when you got tattooed a couple of years ago."

I thought back to the time when I got those tattoos, when I wasn't aware that sex reassignment surgery might be a future option for me. I was looking for a means to affirm my female gender identity. The permanency of a butterfly tattoo was intriguing and offered a physical solution to a complex mental problem that affected me. I regret that I left Madge out of the decision-making, but gender identity has always had an undeniable power over me.

"And then there was that time you were in Boston getting your arms lasered, and you told me you were at the mall," Madge exclaimed.

True again. As far back as three or four years, I was transitioning without even realizing what I was doing. I would often cross-dress on weekends while Madge and the kids were away visiting her mother. Madge knew what I was doing but could tolerate my odd behavior if I kept it private and if we didn't talk much about it. Hair removal from my arms allowed me to wear short-sleeve blouses and look less manly. I reassured Madge that I had never had an affair, and she nodded with acknowledgement.

As I readied for my walk, I asked, "Would it help if I brought Jake back one more time, for a day or so, so people could say good-bye to him. I could find some men's clothes for him to wear, remove my earrings, my nail polish, and my make-up. I could deepen my voice and even drink beer again!"

She looked at me as if ready to accept her loss.

"No, too much has happened. You can't bring him back. He doesn't exist anymore."

In truth, he just escaped to a place where he could rest and not be found. He was tired, depressed, and felt he had little to live for. He was in the middle of his life, and all those things that seemed so important to him when he was younger no longer did. All of his accomplishments meant nothing. Giving his life to me—Jessie—made him happy. I can still call on him from time to time, but mostly I just let him sleep.

Hoping to Keep My Job

All will be well, and all will be well, and all manner of things will be well. This was the theme of our Sunday sermon at the Unitarian Church of Nashua just one week earlier. On most days, it was common for me to question my sanity and feel there were two people in my head, but on this particular day I needed to find the confidence to present only that part of myself that was Jessica Birch. Nothing else could be apparent. This was the day that I was to have psychological testing with Dr. Jukowski in Manchester to determine if I was fit to return to work as a physician. It had been just a little over a year since I first opened up to Dr. Gransby about my gender dysphoria, but it seemed like a decade.

I was dressed professionally for the occasion. I wore a white lace camisole under a white blouse, black INC slacks from Macy's, and a blue dress jacket with a cloth belt that tied in the front. I had my hair done and my nails manicured, and I practiced my voice for over an hour before my appointment.

I wasn't sure what to expect. Would he be knowledgeable or judgmental? What would he think of me? How would I win him over?

For nearly three hours we talked. He was an older gentleman, and he talked softly, wore a white shirt and a bow tie, and seemed like a fair man. He told me at the start that he was being paid by my employer but would try not to let that influence his decision-making. I did my best to present well, and I think I had good answers for his questions.

He asked me about my childhood. I expected that he would. I told him about the difficulties I had growing up, the humiliation I felt in the boy's locker room after gym class, my desires to be a girl since puberty, the love I had for my father, and my mother's harsh nature. I told him how I had been consumed with guilt for so many years and how I couldn't take confession at my father-in-law's funeral. I related how I met Dr. Gransby and later Dr. Braunwald. I wanted him to know everything about me, and I wanted him to be able to enter my soul and feel what I had experienced.

At noon he asked me if I wanted to go to lunch. I went to the cafeteria, ate a tuna sandwich, and returned for a battery of written and computerized personality tests. I figured this part of the testing would be easy until I clicked on a computer question that read: I have thought about suicide recently. (A) True or (B) False. I couldn't lie. I'd spent too much time asking for forgiveness. In addition, Dr. Jukowski told me he was going to review records from Dr. Braunwald and Dr. Gransby. My suicidal ideation would be in those records and lying would only make things worse. I clicked (A).

As I finished the testing, I asked the receptionist if I could speak with the doctor one more time before I left for home. She beckoned to him in his office, received an affirmative reply, and escorted me back. He offered me a seat, and I proceeded to say, "Dr. Jukowski, I need to explain an answer to one of the computerized tests. A question asked if I had recently contemplated suicide, and I checked yes. You need to know that I wouldn't do it. I don't have the courage, and it's against my religious beliefs. I feel that I am ready to return to work, and I think I can be an even better physician than I was before if given the chance. There are a lot of people like me who could use my help. People will hopefully see me for who I am and what I stand for, not that I am a transsexual. If a person is Black or Hispanic, with time, don't you forget their racial differences and learn to see them simply as Joe or Mary?"

Dr. Jukowski looked at me with a half sympathetic eye, thanked me for telling him this, and said he would take it into consideration during his evaluation.

I drove home, and that night I didn't sleep well. My future was in the balance, and I didn't know where I stood. I remembered a church hymn I had downloaded to my computer: "Blessed Spirit of My Life: Hymn no. 86." I started playing it over and over until I finally drifted off to sleep.

I awoke some time later in a cold sweat, my hair, my pillow, and my clothes all drenched. The room was dark, and I wondered if I might still be asleep. That night I thought I saw angels.

They were faceless with long bodies and arms. They surrounded me and together they made an odd noise, like they were softly howling or repeating a chant of some kind. I started crying, and I felt dozens of hands come over me without actually touching me. The more I cried, the louder their voices became, and then they were gone. The next morning, while taking a bath and with my eyes closed, I thought I felt them again, but when I opened my eyes, there was nothing unusual about the room. Was I dreaming, was it my imagination, or was it real? I don't know. It's easy for the brain to play tricks on you when you're emotional state is unbalanced.

Although there were times when I felt confident, strong, full of creativity and vigor, there were other times, especially when I was alone at night, when I'd feel myself sinking, as if into a deep, dark well. When this happened, it would often come on without warning. I'd sense myself trying to peer up out of the well, and I'd have trouble seeing the daylight. My eyes would want to close, I'd feel a lump in my throat, and my breathing would change. I'd have trouble taking a full breath, and I'd feel the need to exhale quickly. Was I depressed, was I feeling the sadness of the world, or might it be that I was feeling the love of God?

I took a moment to contemplate the life of Jesus. He was a great man in his time, and his ideas of love and forgiveness were novel. People wanted to believe that there was a better world, where starvation and disease didn't exist, where robbers and thieves got their due, and where fairness ran supreme. There were no antibiotics, no birth control, and if a person lived to be thirty, they were lucky. Jesus symbolized hope, but greedy politicians and clergy wanted him dead because they feared an uprising of the populace if they let him live.

We know little about his mid-life, but I believe that, just as I was going through some form of transformation, he too experienced some life-altering event. What that event was I don't know, but it provided him with a vision that he felt he had to share with others.

I would never proclaim myself to be his equal. No, far from it, but was there a commonality between us? We had both experienced some injustice in our lives. Was I, too, being called upon to share my life with others?

I prayed, "All Will Be Well."

CHANGING MY VOICE
AND MORE

Melancholy! What is melancholy? I think it's the way I feel. It's being happy and sad at the same time. Jessie makes me happy. I can close my eyes and imagine her and thus become her. I love all the things she can do, the places she can go, the clothes she can wear, and the people she's able to meet. Where does the sadness come from? It comes from losing many of the people I loved in the past, leaving behind a life I once had, and facing the uncertainty of a future not only as a woman but also as a transsexual woman in a world that's not always accepting and forgiving of people who are different. I was told this might happen, and I prepared myself the best I could.

As the metamorphosis evolved, I could sense the transformation. There were times when I felt as if insanity was taking over my being, although I suspect it was just Jessie becoming more and more a part of me. The mental image I had of myself was changing, and I could see physical changes occurring as well. When I looked in the mirror, I noticed that there were basically no hairs on my upper lip; the laser treatments and the one hundred hours or so of electrolysis to date were finally showing their effect. I could see my breasts developing, and my hips appeared wider. I had been taking voice lessons, and I could now speak with a somewhat feminine-sounding voice, although not for any sustained period of time or with any volume intensity initially.

My voice coach, Rhonda, was a marvelous woman who used a keyboard and a computer to help me attain that voice. Unfortunately, estrogen itself, unlike testosterone, cannot change the pitch of your voice. My vocal cords had been thickened by years of testosterone exposure and it was, for the most part, irreversible. What I had to learn now was how to use them differently. Breathing correctly was a big part of that as was drinking plenty of water to stay well hydrated and thus help prevent injury to them. In addition, Rhonda instructed me on how to vary the intonation of my voice and how to make the enunciation of certain vowels and consonants crisper. She had me do something called "upside down girl" where I had to bend over, as if touching my toes, and try to repeat phrases like "Zig Zigler's pizzazz exhilarated the Zambians" and "Many men made millions," all while trying to maintain a voice frequency above 210 hertz. She made audio CDs for me to practice with while driving, and she had me leave voice recordings on her answering machine that she would analyze later. As a final test, she had me call restaurants and ask for reservations without telling the maître d' whether I was a man or woman. I was thrilled when they responded by saying, "And how many will be in your party, ma'am?"

I looked at my male genitals now with some disgust and hated the wideness of my shoulders. When buying a woman's suit consisting of a jacket and a skirt, I had to buy both a size 14 and a size 6, because most clothing manufacturers expect the two pieces to be sold as a set, and I was proportionately bigger on the top than on the bottom. Oddly enough, as a woman, five foot seven is considered tall, but as a guy it's considered short. When I was heavy, my shoe size was a ten and a half or eleven, but after losing fifty pounds, it changed to a size ten. That was a godsend. Most guys probably aren't aware of this, but it's very difficult for women to find shoes larger than a size ten or smaller than a size six. Having my shoe size decrease meant that I could find shoes that would fit me in all the major department stores. So cool!

Did you know that the width of a woman's forehead averages between six and six and a half centimeters, whereas that of a man's is usually greater than seven? Have you noticed that a woman's forehead is generally flat, while a man's usually has a depression in the middle with bossing (a prominent ridge) of the bone over the eyebrows? When a woman smiles, you can usually see her upper teeth but a man's are usually hidden. This is because women generally have a shorter upper lip. In addition, a woman's chin is usually narrow and the jaw more angulated compared to the wide chin and square shape of a man's jaw. These are just a few of the many structural differences between a man's and a woman's face. It's my guess that we are all subconsciously aware of these differences, and we size up a person's virility and mating potential based on these visual perceptions.

Although some people think women are inferior to men, I think it's a privilege to be a woman. There are so many fun things afforded to the female gender, such as adornment of one's self, the freedom to communicate with gestures, and the freedom to express one's emotions.

I don't know what I'd do without my red backpack purse, and I am attached to my PDA with the pink monogrammed leather case. I've developed favorites among the many items in my wardrobe, and I like experimenting with accessories like hats, scarves, watches, and belts.

I've become fairly proficient at applying make-up, and I now know the importance of a good facial cleanser and moisturizer. I've become partial to the Clinique line of women's skin products, and I love their foundation. I know what a "pumpkin mask" is, and I enjoy talking with other women about salons. I've discovered that many manicurists prefer OPI nail polish, and I like the long cap, which makes it easier to hold and apply the polish. Whereas Jake could never understand why women spent so much money on eye products to prevent wrinkles and such, Jessie has a keen appreciation for their value. There are many hair products on the market, and I've learned to welcome their differences; a good conditioner is a must and various mousses, pastes, and gels can each have their place. As for jewelry, an eighteen-inch chain is best for my neck, and I wish more bracelets came in eight-inch lengths as opposed to the typical seven and a half-inch size. A claw clasp on a neck chain is also recommended, because it gives the greatest security against losing an expensive pendant.

All my dreams were coming true. I was becoming the woman I always wanted to be, yet the happiness I had longed for and imagined for so many years was tempered by the sadness of knowing I could never really be a biological woman; I would always be a transwoman. Rather than being grateful for the second chance at life that I was granted, I wanted more.

I didn't want to be someone pretending to be a woman; I wanted to know what it was like to be a sexual woman. I wanted to know why women found childbirth so special, what it felt like to have your breasts engorged with milk, and what it felt like to have a menstrual period. I wanted to be alluring, passionate, and mysterious, someone men found irresistible, yet how could I make that possible when I always felt so insecure about my sexuality. I had no experience. I had no understanding of how to be a sexual woman. I needed to go through female puberty and experience the awkwardness of being a teenage girl, the bond of a mother-daughter relationship, and the rejection as well as the love of a man.

PREJUDICE AND ADVOCACY

No journey is without perils, twists and turns, and unexpected events. While I tried my best to foresee the future, I often miscalculated. A transsexual is an oddity of nature. There are those who find ways to function in society, but many are shunned and treated with indignation. You never know what it actually feels like to be in a minority until you're part of one. In grade school, I remember a game we played to teach us about prejudice. For one week, all of the kids with blue eyes got to sit up front and were granted special privileges, while the kids with brown eyes were made to sit in the back and weren't allowed to speak unless spoken to. The week after, the roles were reversed. It was a clever lesson but still just a game. We always knew the condition was temporary. What happens, though, when you wake up one day and find you're in a similar situation, but it's no longer a game—you're the demoralized one—and it's permanent?

As an example, consider the following:

I was outraged one day when I couldn't get a prescription for estrogen filled at my local pharmacy simply because, according to the computer system and my medical insurance carrier, I was an "M" rather than an "F." Their policies excluded estrogen treatment for men; and vice-versa, testosterone treatment for women on the grounds that "gender identity disorder" was excluded in their policies. It was not enough that my family physician, my psychiatrist, and my endocrinologist all agreed that this was appropriate treatment for me. I thought to myself, "How dare they do this to me! What right did they have to specifically exclude me? If I had a medical diagnosis such as diabetes, high blood pressure, or high cholesterol, appropriate medical treatment wouldn't be excluded." It seemed like such a paradox since people with those medical conditions often make unhealthy choices; their conditions are often preventable; and as patients, they tend to consume the majority of the medical insurance company's resources. Why not exclude them? The simple answer is that two-thirds of Americans are overweight, and how do you exclude a majority of the shareholders?

I decided to take action. I contacted one of the New Hampshire House representatives and pleaded my case. She became sympathetic to my cause, and soon after we put together a bill and requested a congressional hearing. It got the attention of a lot of people, and even though the bill failed to pass, it helped bring the transgender community together, and it helped educate the public.

I remember vividly the day that hearing occurred. We were a ragtag group of societal misfits with a common purpose, and while we waited for the hearing to start, we could hear people laughing in an adjacent hallway. Postings on the walls described various bills that were being presented in different rooms, and ours was the brunt of their laughter. Men in business suits thought it a joke that a bunch of transsexuals could find the courage and the know-how to come to the state house and plead their case.

"Can't they see that they're just wasting their time and the committee members' time?" I thought I overheard one gentleman say.

Less than twenty of us gathered that day, and the three largest insurance companies in the state each sent a representative to plead their case against us. They all sat together, prim and proper, in their dark-colored business suits with their briefcases by their sides. We, on the other hand, looked like a bunch of mismatched socks, but we clamored to be heard. Some wrote their stories on paper and read them aloud. Others chose to speak from their hearts with no preparation. I myself used the skills of my college and medical school education to research an argument of defense. It went like this:

The prevalence of transgendered individuals in the population is not easy to determine. Statistics in the Netherlands from the 1990s estimate 1 per 12,000 males and 1 per 30,000 females is transgendered. Singapore statistics estimate 1 in 9000 males and 1 in 27,000 females. Some suggest an even higher prevalence and possible equality between the sexes. Given that the current population of New Hampshire is roughly 1.4 million, even if we use a prevalence of 1 in 5000, the number of trans- gendered people who might request hormone therapy from their insurance companies is less than 300. Many transgendered people do not want hormone therapy, and they may not consider themselves transsexual. They enjoy cross-dressing but prefer their biological sex. Many probably don't have insurance, and some are likely fear- ful of talking with someone from the medical community about their gender issues. Therefore, it's likely that the true number of people who would request hormone therapy from their insurance company would be even less. Of the ones who would request such treatment, I believe that their medical provider, using the most current treatment guidelines, should manage them. Most practitioners use the standards of care as presented by the World Professional Association for Transgender Health, which typically recommends behavioral health counseling with a therapist trained in gender disorders before hormone therapy is recommended or initiated.

The actual cost of hormone therapy per person per month will vary. For a male to female transsexual, estrogen therapy retails for roughly $25 to $75 per month, depending on brand and delivery system (i.e. pill, patch, sublingual, etc.). Androgens for female to male transsexuals can range from $20 per month for injections to $210 per month for gels. Oral androgens are not recommended. Of course, this is not the price insurance companies would pay, as they typically arrange contracts with distributors for wholesale pricing. In addition, most insurance companies also require the patient to pay for a portion of the cost of their medication in the form of a co-payment.

The insurance company representatives and some of the committee members argued that the cost of health care was already too high and that allowing hormone therapy for a small group of transsexuals didn't warrant the expense. One particular House representative, independently wealthy I believe, was staunchly against us and had no empathy for our cause. I know it's not good of me to think this way, but I wished he could lose his fortune and then develop some horrible disease in which his health insurance company denied him treatment. Then he'd know how we felt.

Interestingly, the small committee who listened to us actually voted in our favor. Unfortunately, the committee's recommendation fell on deaf ears when the vote went to the House.

A certain amount of celebrity status goes along with a physician want- ing a sex change, and although it brought me some disrepute, I liked the attention. I imagined myself in battle, shield dented and flag held high, wounded and lacking armor, charging the enemy with my sword, and leading the army behind me. Whereas one person would say I was sick, another would say I was courageous, and I myself was unsure which group properly portrayed me. Was it selfish of me to want the life I had always dreamed of? I openly proclaimed myself transgendered and invited the local newspaper to interview me. To the dismay of my employer, I wrote letters to the editor and was once featured on the front page of the Sunday *Telegraph*. My oldest boy almost disowned me for that, but I've always been idealistic, and I convinced myself that no sacrifice for transgender rights was too great and to hush my voice and not speak out would be a betrayal of my moral values. What example would I set for my son if I cowered to public pressure?

But wasn't it also possible that I was trying to make a name for myself, that I enjoyed being the center of attention, and that I was justifying the importance of my own existence?

I was in a quandary and didn't know which to be true.

When Chaz Bono came out publicly as being transgendered, I wrote to CNN in support of him, and they contacted me and asked me if I would be willing to do an Internet talk radio show. I was thrilled. How exciting it seemed to be associated with Chaz Bono. I gave little thought to the possibility that friends or family might hear or see the show, but the interview was available for viewing on the main page of the CNN website for days on end.

It was not long before my son Jonathan found out. My claim to fame was short-lived. Jonathan refused to invite me to his high school graduation. Of course, I went to the graduation anyway, hiding in a back row seat, unable to get my picture taken with him or sit with any of our relatives. Even my therapist Dr. Braunwald questioned my motive for doing the show. I wish now that my decision had been different, but as it's often said, you can never go back. I have to live with what I did. Maybe the punishment should have been worse.

I reconciled with Jonathan about a year later, but we still struggled for quite some time after that to be as close as we once were.

As time passed, and the country went into a recession, people forgot about those newspaper articles, and instead they focused on housing and the job market. The transgender community of New Hampshire faded out of the limelight, and I settled into a life less infamous.

THOUGHTS, TRUTH, AND HONESTY

On the way home from the New England Gender Conference, while driving on Route 495 north, tears welled up, and I couldn't stop them from streaming down the side of my cheek. I had realized who I was and had found freedom from the devil within me, but it was not without a cost. Never again would I spend the night in the house of my dreams, the home that I bought with a loan from the Veteran's administration, just as my dad had done some thirty years before me. Madge and my children would forever be affected by my actions, and no amount of rationalization about the necessity to change would lessen my sense of selfishness. Happiness was an illusion, yet being true to myself, recognizing that evolution and the supremacy of the universe had made the decision to place inside me a sexual blueprint that was damaged, was undeniable. Had I the chance to see my future, I still would have wanted to live my life as a girl. My desire to be female was as much a part of me as the freckles on my nose. In many cultures, women are devalued and looked down upon as being less advantaged, but in my mind the female gender is so much more expressive, gentler in nature, and freer to live life without inhibitions. I desired nothing less than to live the rest of my life as a woman. It meant everything to me.

I felt better as the tears wetted my face, like the pressure being released from a steam valve that had reached the red zone. If I had held it back any longer, my pipes would surely have burst.

The night before, I had driven to my parent's home in Bernardston, Massachusetts. They had agreed to let me stay with them while I attended a three-day conference on gender diversity in Northampton, Massachusetts. During my stay, they were very nice to me, and they even tried to remember to call me Jessie. I'm sure they pondered the idea that I might be experiencing some form of temporary insanity, but they loved me and didn't want to cause me any harm.

I've read that you shouldn't wake a sleepwalker or someone having a bad dream; instead, you should just keep them safe. Who knows, maybe a gender identity crisis isn't much different.

My parents were wonderful that weekend. My dad gave up his bed for me and slept on the couch. In the morning, both my mom and my dad made sure I ate breakfast and advised me to drive carefully on my way to the conference. I think we all felt a little awkward, but that was to be expected. Many of the transgendered persons I know struggle with parental acceptance. I consider myself fortunate in that regard. My parents have never ridiculed me or made me feel unwanted.

The conference was for health professionals, mainly therapists, who provided treatment for transgendered clients. I've been to many medical conferences over the years, but they were always geared toward some topic that was only relevant to me in my work as a family physician, such as heart disease, orthopedic injuries, diabetes, or pediatric concerns—nothing personal.

The lecturers spoke to the audience about their experiences taking care of transgendered clients. They talked about stages of development, therapeutic goals, hormone therapy readiness, and surgery. They talked as if they had special expertise in providing mental health counseling for this unique population of patients, which of course they did, but I couldn't help feeling a little indignant toward them. I went to the conference as a physician, but I was also the one with the disease, the gender identity disorder that required some form of treatment. I felt oddly out of sync there. Only a few of the attendees were actually transgendered. All of the discovery I had gone through in the past two years—the anguish, the shame, the turmoil—I had to relive it again and again. Why was it that I was in medical practice for twelve years before I heard the term transgendered?

My therapist, Dr. Braunwald, was at the conference, too, but because of her therapeutic relationship with me, she couldn't sit with me or carry on an in-depth conversation with me. This further added to my sorrow, but I understood the ethical dilemma she faced, and I did my best to respect her wishes. It was awkward to have her, Jessie the transsexual, and Dr. Mathewson all in the same room at the same time. It was as if at any moment *worlds would collide,* a term I first heard on the TV show *Seinfeld,* during an episode when the show's writers did a spoof about Elaine (the show's heroine) meeting up with three strange men who had habits and behaviors that were just like her three male co-stars. She feared what would happen should they all meet. I felt the same way seeing Dr. Braunwald outside of her office.

One night there was a guest speaker at the conference, and my mom and I went together to hear the lecture. The presenter was Jennifer Boylan, the transgendered English professor from Colby College who had been on *The Oprah Winfrey Show.* She was rather tall and had beautiful long blond hair, and she was very entertaining. She was definitely a positive role model for the transgender community. She was there in part to promote her book *She's Not There: A Life in Two Genders.* I read it twice before hearing her speak, and I enjoyed it immensely. Before we left, I had her sign my copy.

Afterward, on the ride home, my mom and I talked. We discussed the weather (it was snowing that night), we talked about the lecture, and at some point she asked the question I knew she would eventually get around to asking. "Are you sure you want to do this? It will be permanent you know."

Obviously she was speaking of my planned gender reassignment surgery. I replied with the answer she knew I would, "Yes, Mom, I'm sure. I'm just like Jennifer Boylan, the lady we heard speak tonight. I know it must seem strange to you."

"Is it something I did?" my mother queried.

"No, Mom. You didn't cause it. I was just born this way," I replied.

She sighed, and I could tell she doubted my words. She must have felt some guilt over the way she treated me as a child; otherwise, why would she have tried to reconcile her relationship with me? Her belief that she was the sole cause of my gender conflict is not likely true. The complex orchestra of chemical mediators and hormone signals generated by my DNA were performing a symphony, and they were entrusted with the ultimate goal of creating something female. How environmental triggers might be a part of that process is a mystery.

Anyway, she looked different. The angry woman screaming at me as a child, cursing me as if I should never have been born, was no longer there. Instead, the person sitting next to me seemed to carry her own sadness. There was a look of compassion in her facial expressions that I'd never seen before. What did I really know about her? She once told me that her brother had drowned when he was only four years old. He was playing in the back-yard near a river and his paddleball must have gone in the water and he went after it. They had to dredge the river to find his body. How horrible that must've been for her. She didn't talk about it a lot, probably because it was too painful, but was my misfortune really any more tragic than hers?

It was one of the first times I ever felt like I could talk to my mother. I never remember having any private discussions with her as a child. She was different now. There was a human side to her that that she no longer wanted to hide from me. I found it hard to open up to her fully, but it was a start.

On the ride home, she said she was worried about me and she feared someone might hurt me, and she told me in her own way that she loved me.

It was time to start forgiving and to start healing the wounds I had suffered so many years ago. It was time to let go of the past and find peace in the present.

SURGERY IN MONTREAL

It was May 2007 and my surgery date was less than a week away. As I finished some last minute packing, Pam called to let me know she was leaving and she would pick me up soon for the drive to Montreal. That's where I had arranged to have my gender reassignment surgery with Dr. Yvon Menard. The trip would take about eight hours. Had we not stopped a few times along the way, we could have made it in five and a half.

Pam arrived excited to see me, and I couldn't believe that what I'd dreamed of all my life was soon to happen. It was like waiting for Christmas. If you thought about it too much, it seemed an eternity for the day to finally come. I wanted Pam to have a good time, so I focused my efforts on making the trip enjoyable for her. After all, thinking about someone else's happiness is always better than thinking about your own.

Only thirty minutes outside of Nashua, we found ourselves hungry. After a brief drive through the center of Manchester, we agreed to eat at an Italian restaurant on the east side. It was a beautiful day with no humidity and only a few clouds. The restaurant had a veranda, so we chose to eat outside at a table in partial sun with an umbrella. After perusing the menu, we made our selection and decided to split a meal of salmon and linguine with a sauce of mushrooms, capers, and lemon. It was delicious. Once we finished eating and after having an iced tea, we couldn't help but find humor in the fact that two and a half hours had passed, and we'd only traveled twenty miles.

After leaving the restaurant, we took turns driving and dozing until we reached Montpelier, Vermont. Montpelier is the smallest capital in the United States, and rather than a city, it's more like a quaint village with one main street, a few small stores and boutiques, a movie theater, and a couple of cafés. The Capital building is on Main Street, and it's notable for a large tulip garden lining both sides of a masonry pathway leading to its front steps. We stopped, took some pictures, and then walked to one of the outdoor cafés, sat at a small table on the walkway, enjoyed a margarita, and ate some taco chips.

We only stopped one more time, after passing through customs and within miles of Montreal. The sun was setting, and the sky was a beautiful mix of pink, yellow, and red, while the land was flat and dotted with farmhouses. We pulled over and took several pictures, delighting ourselves in the moment and hoping we could capture it on film.

We reached Montreal during early evening, and the metropolis seemed vast with many intersecting highways and buildings with bright lights. As we passed over the St. Lawrence River, the dark currents below were still visible, and I could hear the sound of the car wheels echo as we rumbled into the city.

Once we were in the downtown area, I couldn't help but notice all of the stores, the streets bustling with pedestrians, and the frequent honking of car horns. We found a nice hotel, and I went in to arrange a room while Pam waited in the car outside.

"Bonjour, madame," the hotel registrar said to me.

I politely asked if she could speak English and told her I was looking for a room for two people.

"Would you like one bed or two? It will be the same price whichever you choose."

I wanted so much to say, "One bed please," for I longed to be as close to Pam physically as I felt emotionally. A vestige of my male self and a preoperative resurgence of testosterone, secondary to the required stopping of estrogen three weeks previously, likely contributed to my amorous desires.

Different scenarios played themselves out in my head, and I let my imagination explore all of the possibilities. I could say to her, "There's a room available, but we'll have to share a double bed." This however would be dishonest.

Pam was heterosexual, and she couldn't see Jacob, the man within me. She only saw Jessie. I was a woman to her, even if I still had my male parts. I cared too much about her feelings to present myself falsely, and so with a heartfelt sigh, I said to the registrar, "A room with two beds please."

After checking in and finding ourselves pleased with the accommodations, we decided to go to the casino located on a small island off the St. Lawrence River. The last time I had been to a casino was about thirty years prior when I spent a day in Reno while on leave from the US Air Force. Pam gambled at casinos a few times a year, and she was anxious to show me the ropes. It was a very clean casino, smoke free, and not crowded, as it was a weekday. The other players were generally friendly, and I imagined myself in a James Bond movie with those around me involved in some spy plot that involved intrigue and espionage. I was the femme fatale.

I had some small winnings at roulette, broke even at craps, and lost at the blackjack tables. Pam ended up ahead with winnings of about $130, which were mostly from a silly slot machine we referred to as "Larry the Lobster." The object of the game was to get lucky enough to go to a bonus round where you could cast your line for fish of different monetary values while trying to avoid catching a lobster. I sat and watched as she played, and we laughed about the least little thing, as we were both a little giddy from lack of sleep.

When we arrived back at the hotel, it was close to morning and our comic behavior continued as we each tried to open the door to our room using our casino card rather than the key card given to us by the hotel registrar. When we realized our stupidity, we both looked at each other with our mouths wide open and our eyes agape, and burst into laughter.

Once in the room, and after changing into our pajamas, we had a further laugh when we couldn't figure out how to turn the entrance light off. Oddly it was triggered by the opening and closing of the closet door, and as if in a Laurel and Hardy skit, by the sheer luck of one of us closing that door, we were finally able to retire for the evening.

We fell asleep quickly, each in our own bed. At times, while Pam slept, I would look over at her. I took special note of how she positioned herself, how her face and hair looked, and how she occasionally laughed out loud while dreaming. I imagined lying next to her, feeling her warmth, and kissing her gently while alternatively opening and closing my eyes. Out of necessity, and to avoid breaking the bond of trust between us, I needed to tame my heart and console my sexual desires, for I was a transsexual, an alien to mankind. I was someone whose spiritual essence reached out to others, craving to be loved, but because I was neither male nor female, someone who belonged to the middle sex, physical love was elusive.

The next day, after arising late and greeting Pam with a cheerful good morning, I thought of all the fun things we might do together that day, like shopping, taking in the sights, and enjoying good food and spirits. It was a bright sunny day, and we had enough time before check out to take a swim in the hotel's outdoor heated pool. The air was crisp, and Pam and I found ourselves alone, splashing in the water, our voices echoing through the tall buildings surrounding us. It was such a refreshing way to start the day, and it reminded me of the essay I once wrote as part of the Brandeis University application process. Both stories involved women, the life sustaining properties of water, and the ability of non-living objects to act as witnesses to our life experience.

I felt a sense of satiety and warmth as Pam and I savored the day. I enjoyed being just her friend. We were two girls out on the town. The female in me was now dominant, and I thought to myself, "If I do have a split personality, each of a separate gender so to speak, then there must also be a third entity within me that's not gender specific and has no primal urges, an entity that heeds to a higher power, one that negotiates for truth and all that can be good within me, while calling on the individual strengths of man and woman."

What a wonderful day we had shopping and taking in the sights. We bought some things we probably didn't need, had a grand time sipping a mid-day martini on the second floor balcony of a cozy café on Crescent Street, and had a late afternoon appetizer at a Chinese restaurant.

We had checked out of our hotel earlier in the day, and it was time for Pam and I to find our new temporary residence. My surgeon had made arrangements for me to stay at a bed and breakfast in Laval, a suburb of Montreal. Prior to our departure, I had communicated with the hostess, Brigitte, that I would be arriving a few days early and I would be bringing a friend who would also need a room. She was able to accommodate us, and I was greatly relieved to know that we had a relatively inexpensive place to stay close to the hospital.

For someone familiar with Montreal, the bed and breakfast was a twenty-minute ride from downtown Montreal, but for us, because we got lost, it turned out to be a three-hour test of emotions. It's true, we had directions, but once we made one mistake, we were bound for disaster. I was actually the calm one, the pacifist trying to absorb the tension, as Pam drove. We eventually called Brigitte for help, convinced her of our desperation, parked on a side street, and waited for her to come and find us. She was a great host. When she arrived to our rescue, she hugged us and empathized with us regarding our frustrations. She asked her husband, Yves, to follow us in their car to the bed and breakfast, while she rode with us, giving directions.

Their home was charming with five bedrooms on two separate floors, a good-sized kitchen, a den, and a fenced in backyard. They had a small table and chairs situated next to a garden fountain shaped like a small pond. The bedrooms had their own unique décor. Pam took the only one on the first floor, and I chose a spacious one with a private shower and bath on the second floor. Brigitte loved art and enjoyed painting. Her work, although amateur, showed a great deal of effort and brightened the downstairs rooms. The kitchen was a gathering area for guests, and Brigitte cooked not only breakfast but also lunch and supper for us. Her meals were delicious, and she used a variety of spices, herbs, fruits, and organic vegetables.

By the time Pam and I settled in for our second night in Montreal, it was well after ten o'clock, and we were famished. With the help of Brigitte, we found a late-night diner not far from our residence where we gorged on steak, shrimp, and wine. When we were done, we both felt like we overate, but we also felt some contentment knowing that the evening wasn't a total wash.

Back at the bed and breakfast, we had another glass of wine in my upstairs bedroom. I then lay on the bed, fully clothed, with my head on the pillow. Pam stood off to one side, awkwardly gazing and fixating on objects around the room. I felt the male in me pressing to speak, soon to be no more, wanting one last chance to voice its desires. With burgeoning testosterone flowing through me, compounded by alcohol, I tried to tell Pam how much I enjoyed her company. I wanted to kiss her or just lay with her in a semi-dark room, exploring thoughts with her while eyeing the ceiling or listening to soft music.

Strangely, it was not sex but intimacy I wanted. Pam sat on the edge of the bed but kept her distance, sending me a silent message that she cared about me but she couldn't give me that part of herself she reserved for a "real" man, not someone who presented as a woman and was soon to be castrated. With the help of that rational being within me, again negotiating a truce between my male and female self, I figuratively bowed with head down to the beauty of love and the sadness of truth. Pam wished me good night, turned off the light, and quietly left. I lay staring around the room for a few minutes before falling to sleep, trying to stay strong, rationalizing my existence as a gentle tear rolled down my cheek.

The next morning I awoke and went downstairs to join others already seated in the kitchen. I laughed and joked with them while Pam still slept. I put the events of the night before out of my mind, and when Pam eventually came to breakfast, I presented myself joyfully, blocking Jacob from expressing any signs of sorrow, hoping for another fun and eventful day.

After breakfast, we began our last full day together by taking a visit to a health food store that had some unique foods and supplements. Pam, being very knowledgeable about these types of stores, always made grocery shopping an adventure. Before I met her, my meals were uneventful and bland. Now I drank and ate things like pomegranate juice, ginger tea, hummus, veggie burgers, and mangos. That day, I bought bran fiber cereal and real cocoa. They would easily keep until I left for home, and they were also unbreakable. Pam, on the other hand, bought many more items to bring home, and as I watched her load them in her car, I felt a little sad knowing she would be leaving me in another day.

After our brief food-shopping excursion, we went to a large indoor mall and spent most of our time there at an upscale women's cosmetic store. The sales ladies were all dressed in black and wore aprons lined with make-up brushes. They looked über professional. What a great time we had getting our faces made up—lips, eyebrows, and eyelids mainly. I was so excited, and I loved the attention. All the colors were so pretty. Purple was not purple but Velvet Goddess. I was a woman. I was Jessie having a grand time with one of my best friends.

Jacob was there also and excited, too! I knew this because I had to hide an erection. It was embarrassing, and I wanted it to go away. I didn't want to be male, and I found myself struggling to define my gender. I commanded the female within me to dominate. I felt happiest this way. I wanted Jessie's innocence, her love of life, beauty, and compassion to encompass my being and allow me to treasure this moment. After we left the store, I tried to tell Pam about what had been going on in my head, but I could sense the concept was difficult for her to comprehend, and so I dropped the discussion and redirected my thoughts back to shopping, eating, and having fun.

JESSICA ANGELINA BIRCH

That night, our last evening together, we both wanted to go to Gibby's restaurant in Old Montreal, as it's known for being one of the finest restaurants in the city. We arrived late and had difficulty finding it as well as a place to park. We were worried that without reservations we might not be able to get a table; however, arriving late worked to our advantage. Even though it was a Saturday night, most people had already dined and had left to enjoy the rest of the evening. For this reason, or possibly just dumb luck, we were seated and were not disappointed. The waitress brought bread and pickles to our table as a starter, and we ordered a bottle of wine. For the main course, we both chose fish. I had the sea bass and Pam the arctic char. My meal was delicious, and she seemed to enjoy hers as well. We finished our dining experience with one of those alcoholic beverages the waiter lights on fire and serves with a sweet, frothy topping.

We left the restaurant sometime after midnight, around closing time. As we walked down some wide cement steps toward the street, a most unexpected event occurred. Four well-dressed businessmen approached us, and one began talking. He said something about the nice night, explained they were from out of town and looking to go dancing or find a party, and asked if we two lovely ladies would like to join them. No sooner than I could process what the man had said, Pam blurted out, "Sure, we were thinking of finding a place to dance or have a drink, too." I couldn't believe what was happening. I was being picked up.

Part of me was extremely frightened, but another part of me wanted to know if I could pull it off, if these handsome men could accept me as a woman, and what the experience would be like. My curiosity won out, but the effects of drink as well as Pam's extroverted personality helped. I tried to let her do most of the talking, as I felt terribly insecure, and I wasn't sure what I should say or do.

At one point, when the men were busy talking among themselves and a safe distance away from us, I whispered to Pam, "I don't think I can do this. What if they find out about me?"

To this she replied, "Oh, just put more lip gloss on and laugh a lot. You'll be fine!"

Oh my God, what was I about to do! That's all I kept thinking to myself. Luckily, it was dark, and the men seemed mostly fixated on Pam. I think they saw me as her less attractive, timid sidekick. One of the men, the one who seemed most at ease with women and whose name was Carl, suggested that we hail a couple of cabs to take us into the night club section of old Montreal. His business associates, along with Pam, agreed with the proposal, and soon I found myself riding in a taxi miles from the restaurant. Carl seemed nice, commented about male chivalry, and paid the cab driver when we arrived at our destination. We were now with four big men who we didn't know, in a strange city far from home, after midnight, and with no transportation. Was I insane to let this happen?

No sooner did we exit the cab along a narrow cobblestone street than some people from a second-floor apartment yelled down to us, requesting that we come up and join their party. We advanced across the street and up a flight of stairs while following some strangers. It all seemed so unreal to me, and I couldn't help but think about my surgery that was only two days away. I couldn't afford to do anything stupid and have something bad happen to me that would cause it to be delayed.

It's not easy to have gender reassignment surgery. You need to have a letter of recommendation from a therapist who has experience treating gender identity disorders. In addition, you need to have two more letters, one from a physician and another from a different medical or allied health professional, supporting your perceived need for the surgery. You're also required to be on hormone therapy for at least a year, and at the time I had my surgery, you had to pass a *real life test*, which meant you presented yourself to others, both at home and at work, for one year in the gender you planned to transition to.

Too much was at stake for me. I had to keep my wits about me. I needed to avoid drinking any more alcohol, and I needed to convince Pam to leave with me as soon as possible. Unfortunately, she didn't look like she wanted to leave any time soon. It was going to be difficult to get her out of this place; the men were attractive, and she was in the mood for dancing.

Upstairs in the apartment, it was relatively dark, with just one dim table lamp in a small room adjoining the kitchen and living room. No walls separated the rooms, and in the small kitchen off to one side, a few men were making drinks, and the counter was full of liquor bottles. In the living room a young man was spinning CDs while two others played the bongos. The place was noisy, not only from the music but also from the commotion of people mingling, talking, and dancing. It was smoky but the windows were wide open, and the street below was fairly quiet.

I was scared, and I tried to avoid communication with anyone. I didn't wander far from Pam, who was flirting with two of the men we came with. She was also getting tipsy, and I sensed we were vulnerable. During most of the first hour, I stayed glued to the wall next to the kitchen. One of the men who came with us—the good-looking one who accompanied us in the cab—worked his way over to me and started a conversation. Presenting himself as a gentleman, he told me he worked for a company that made organic foods, and when I told him I was a physician, he began talking about a hernia surgery he had during high school. He proceeded to tell me how his right testicle had gotten large, and I sensed he was trying to find a way to turn the conversation toward sex. I felt clammy, and I'm sure he could see the fear in my eyes. He brought me a drink from the kitchen, which tasted like pure liquor with a splash of soda water. He got one for Pam, too! I pretended to drink mine, and when the timing was right, I found a secluded spot where I could talk to Pam. "We have to go. They're trying to get us drunk."

To this she replied, "Oh, they just want to have fun. Nothing will happen to us. Come on, let's dance."

She motioned for me to put my purse down with hers, which I did, and then I slowly walked to the center of the living room where other people were dancing. I felt so conflicted. Underneath my pretty outfit and my padded bra was a body with a penis. Would I project that to others while I danced? My feet started moving, slowly at first, then faster as the rest of my body followed. "I need to be Jessie!" I repeated to myself.

As if I was doing relaxation exercises, I concentrated on my hair, then my make-up, then I made myself aware of my bra, my pretty top with the flouncy short sleeves, and my high heels. I was there. I was free to be me with no thoughts of penises or any other form of masculinity. The people in the room became a blur, and I absorbed myself in the music. It felt wonderful!

As time went on, my chest started to hurt from lack of sleep combined with all of the smoke I was breathing in. I really wanted to go home, and it was 3 a.m. One of the men who came with us, a short Spanish looking gentleman with a dress sweater, saw me look over at him, and he winked.

My God, he winked at me!

I turned away quickly, afraid to address his interest. Pam was pretty drunk at this point, and one of the other men who came with us asked her if we girls wanted to continue the party at their hotel. That was it. We needed to get out of there. I grabbed our purses and told Pam it was time to go. She didn't fight me, and soon we were walking down the stairs to the street. It was quiet outside. I had no idea how far we were from our car or in what direction we

should go. We started walking down narrow cobblestone streets along old buildings that were close together. I could hear my breath, and the air was cool. Old Montreal was asleep. Pam was oblivious to any peril we might face as I turned to her and said, "That was the scariest thing I've ever done. If any of those men had found out about me, I could have been beaten up or even killed."

Pam replied, "No, they just wanted to have fun. I'd have told you if I thought we were in any danger."

I mused, "And so said one sheep to another while the wolf eyed its prey."

Luckily, we were walking in the right direction, and I started to recognize some of the streets. Our car was parked near a firehouse not far from the restaurant where we ate. I spotted a cab driver and asked him how far it was to Gibby's. At first he offered to drive us there, but when we learned our destination was only two blocks away, we decided we could walk.

Soon everything became familiar. There was Gibby's in front of us, and the firehouse sat across the street. I spotted our car, and after sighing with relief, I remarked, "Thank God. Now we just have to figure out how to get back to the bed and breakfast."

As I looked over at Pam, she was wobbling and swaying to and fro. Oblivious to the world, she perused her surroundings and then turned toward me, trying to appear diplomatic. Painted on her face was a huge grin, and as I stared toward her, waiting for a response, she burst out laughing. Drink had made everything seem funny to her. Knowing Pam was in no position to make decisions, I advised her that I should drive.

All the way home, every time I would say, "I think it's this way," Pam would start laughing and say, "You don't know where you're going; we're lost."

Two hours later, and after driving over some of the same streets many times, we finally made it back to the bed and breakfast. In retrospect, the whole evening had been comical, an adventure, an experience that colored one of the most important events in my life, yet the outcome could have been tragic. Thank God it was the former.

It was now close to sunrise. I parked the car across the street from the bed and breakfast, and we walked into the house. Pam was still laughing about things only she found humorous, and I was struggling to keep my eyes open. I walked her to her room, asked if she was going to be OK, looked into her eyes, kissed her on the forehead, and said, "Good night."

I turned away quickly, so as not to let myself try to take advantage of her, and went upstairs to my room. I found it difficult to fall asleep, as my chest still burned from cigarette smoke, and my body felt abused from the effects of staying awake too long and drinking too much alcohol. We both awoke sometime in late morning. We showered, had lunch, and said heartfelt good-byes to each other.

That night I was alone with my hosts Brigitte and Yves. The three of us had a splendid dinner together, including bread and cheese fondue, pork, and fresh vegetables. After dinner, we listened to French café music and philosophized about life. Yves, who spoke mainly French interpreted by Brigitte, talked widely about many topics. I sensed goodness in him and caught a glimpse of what may have brought him and Brigitte together. At one point, I learned they enjoyed ballroom dancing and had taken some lessons in the winter. Brigitte demonstrated some of what they had learned, and soon we were moving the kitchen table aside so all three of us could dance and practice the rumba.

I was immersed in the moment, practicing my own dance steps, when we heard a knock on the front door. It was my surgeon. Per his usual routine, he came to the bed and breakfast to visit his patients the night before they were to be transferred to the hospital for their surgery. He was very polite, and he asked me to go upstairs with him to my room where he could talk to me about my surgery. I didn't really have many questions for him, other than to know how he planned to modify my upper lip to give it a more feminine appearance. He explained the procedure to me and then asked if I wanted saline or silicone breast implants. After listening to the pros and cons of both, I chose the silicone ones. He explained the genital surgery briefly and advised me that upon awakening from surgery I would have a vaginal stent and a catheter.

After he left, I retired early and reflected on my life and my transition. Was I selfish, as Marge had suggested to me a few weeks earlier? From her standpoint I was a person who was no longer willing to sacrifice himself for the happiness of the family he helped create. To this, I would have to say I was selfish, and I truly regret any harm I caused.

From my point of view, it was simply self-preservation. I needed to free the part of me that was Jessie; that spirited life within me wanting to explore love, art, new foods, dance, and culture. It wasn't fair to deny her life any longer. I was tired of the long hours at work, the daily stress, the boredom of each day seeming just like the one before it, and the realization that I was getting older and I was horribly unhappy. I was living in a black-and-white movie, and I wanted it to be color.

To expand a little, I don't think the character of our lives can be captured in a single snapshot, but rather our thoughts and actions are fluid; their meaning can change. Someone who sees you at one point in time, without prior reference, can only see who you are at the moment. For those who knew you previously, their image of you can be quite different, as it's a composite of many snapshots overlapping with time. Good and bad are relative terms, and in the end we must judge for ourselves if our life has had meaning, if we've had a purposeful life, and if we're satisfied with the outcome.

As a child brought up Catholic, I often heard it said that the body is a temple of the Holy Spirit. I in no way wanted to offend God, but I was about to surgically alter mine. It was what I needed to do to become whole, but it would forever change me.

The next day, I was transferred to the hospital by taxi. I unpacked, adjusted to my surroundings, and had lunch. It was my last meal before surgery. That night I did the usual prep routine, and they gave me a sedative to help with sleep.

The next morning, a nurse came into my room and said, "It's time, Jessica. Will you follow me?" I undressed, put my surgical gown and booties on, and walked with her to the elevator and up to the second floor of the Centre Métropolitain de Chirurgie Plastique.

From there I was instructed to hop up onto a wheeled table. She covered me with a sheet and told me the anesthesiologist would be with me shortly. When he arrived, he asked me a few questions, started an IV, and then proceeded to push me gently down the hallway. I remember thinking, "This is it. I'm finally here! All my life I've dreamed of this moment." A mask was placed over my face, I was instructed to breath, and then everything went dark. I awoke to a poorly lit room that had a streak of light peaking in from the side of a long vertical window. I could hear the voices of two women speaking to each other in French, and I suspected they were nurses. At some point someone stuck something in my arm, and I surmised that I had been injected with a painkiller. I was semi-oblivious to my surroundings, but I was mindful that the surgery was over and that I felt helpless. No matter which way I moved, I was in pain, and I couldn't sit or roll to either side.

As I became more fully awake, the first thing I noticed was that I had rather large breasts. They were firm and symmetrical. The surgical incisions were located below each breast and would be barely noticeable in years to come. My upper lip was a little sore, too, but not bad. I expected to find an incision inside my mouth, but there was none. It would be another day before I'd have access to a hand mirror so I could see the beautiful work my surgeon did shortening the width of my upper lip while also turning it up to give it a more feminine appearance.

I turned my attention to my genitals. A large bloody gauze was present where my penis used to be, and the dressing was kept in place with stockinet underwear. This was the area that hurt the most. I felt the need to urinate, but the nurse at my bedside, sensing my anxiety, showed me the catheter that lay across my left thigh.

At that point, I knew the operation was complete, and it was now time for me to concentrate on my recovery. The surgery itself was anti-climactic. At the convalescent home, I did what I needed to do to recover and return home. On the fourth post-operative day, my vaginal stent was removed, and I was able to move more freely. My friends from the Unitarian Church of Nashua sent me beautiful flowers, and a number of other people sent me cards. Regretfully, my parents and family couldn't share in my happiness. They were too conflicted. They didn't want to be a part of this celebration; to express any sense of joy regarding my decision for a sex change affirmed that Jacob no longer existed.

Once back in Nashua, I took more time off to fully recuperate before returning to work. My days were occupied by sitz baths, frequent vaginal dilations, and more electrolysis. I have a fairly high pain tolerance, so it wasn't long before I was back to my daily routine.

About a year later, I learned of a surgeon in Boston who did facial feminization surgery. Feeling there was still more to do, I had him operate on me. He reconstructed my forehead and pulled my hairline down, changed the angle of my jaw, narrowed my chin, and subsequently did a facelift. If that wasn't enough, I went back to him a third time for a laser skin resurfacing procedure under general anesthesia. It was a procedure that basically made you look like you'd been though a forest fire, but once healed, my skin was tighter and had a more youthful appearance.

All in all, the few years leading up to and including my surgery had been a journey of emotional and physical changes, but I was finally at a point where I felt there was nothing more I needed to do except live. In some ways, however, that became the hardest part of all.

MOVING ON

L ife after surgery brought new challenges. I was on my own again and was soon to be divorced. I hated living by myself. Many nights, I felt overwhelmingly sad. Would I ever have a family again? Had I traded one sadness for another?

I reasoned that having some company might help me, so I decided to buy a puppy. I was living in a mobile home park, and I was allowed to have one pet, although it couldn't weigh more than twenty-five pounds. "What about a Chihuahua?" I thought. I could take that size dog with me any-where, and it seemed like such a cool pet for a girl to own.

Based on a friend's recommendation, I drove to a pet store in Manchester, New Hampshire, one afternoon in search of the perfect playmate. I saw a pup all alone in one of the cages, a little Yorkie, not a Chihuahua, and she couldn't have been more than a couple of months old. She was so cute. The store manager saw me eyeing her and asked if I wanted to play with her.

"Sure. I'd love to. You wouldn't mind?"

A Yorkie, I hadn't thought of a dog like that, but when I used my imagination, I could see us making a great pair. "It's all about image," I told myself, "and this little dog and I would be a perfect together."

He took her out of the cage and handed her over to me. Then he showed me a small cubicle where I could play with her. She was so soft and cuddly. I didn't want to leave without her.

"How much does she cost?" I asked.

"She's one thousand dollars, and that includes all of her shots," said the manager.

How could I not take her home with me? I thought of all the fun we could have playing tug-of-war and walking in the woods. She fit in the palm of my hand and weighed less than seven pounds.

"I'll...I'll take her!"

"OK, but you can't take her tonight because the veterinarian needs to fully immunize her."

My heart sank. I would have to wait another whole day to take her home. I could hardly sleep that night. I couldn't wait to leave work the next day and go pick her up.

What would I call her? It couldn't be something ordinary. At first I thought about naming her Trixie and experimented with that for about a half day but decided I didn't want her to be considered a tramp amongst other dogs, so I chose a more upstanding name—Abby.

The first night we were together, she cuddled right up to me, and we quickly became friends. I bought a puppy carrier bag to lug her around in, one with a zippered screen window on the side so she could see out of it, and brought her everywhere I went. When I took her to Macy's, all the salesladies loved her. If I forgot to bring a discount coupon and brought her with me, they'd give me the discount anyway, as long as they could hold her.

That first year we were together, she was a lifesaver for me. Throughout the winter, when it was dark and cold, she kept me company. I would get so depressed sometimes, but holding her was comforting, and I enjoyed taking care of her.

Not that my life was always sad, but an undercurrent of sorrow seemed to run through me, and what was layered on the top was a facade. I tried to project a sense of invincibility, an image of a person who accomplished whatever she set out to do, but I was susceptible to emotional breakdowns. I wanted people to think I could conquer armies, but a broken soul stood behind that shield of mine. I carried that hurt with me every day. I had so many losses to bear and so many heartaches I couldn't forget. I felt like I had more than the average person's share of traumas in my life. How was I to ever find someone who could understand my loneliness?

There is this theory, purported by some, that many male-to-female transsexuals are "autogynephilic," meaning they are sexually attracted to the image of themselves as female ("love of one's self as a woman"). Some even develop a sexual interest in men because they want to take on a woman's sexual role with a man; I suppose the latter statement refers to me.

Shortly after my divorce, in the spring of 2008, I met Calvin while walking Abby around my neighborhood. Calvin and I lived in the same trailer park, and he was outside gardening one day when I walked by.

"That's a nice tomato plant you have there. Do you like to grow things?" I inquired, trying to strike up a conversation.

"Oh, hi!" He stopped what he was doing and headed toward me. "Nice to meet you. My name is Calvin. That's a cute dog you have there."

"Thanks. Her name is Abby. I live one street over and around the corner from here. Have you lived here long?"

"A little over a year now, I think. What's your name?"

Thus began our friendship. Calvin was six foot two, thin, and muscular, and he had a partial beard. He liked photography, and he once had his own portrait studio. We both were recently divorced.

I would often walk Abby around the block, hoping he'd be outside, and when he was, sometimes he'd join us for our walk; other times we'd just chat for a bit out on his lawn or in the driveway. We talked about photography, dance, our work, and anything else that popped into our heads.

He was handsome but oddly mysterious. In the beginning, I could never quite tell how much he liked me. Once we went blueberry picking and had a wonderful time, but then I didn't hear from him again for months.

Time marched forward, and I had many adventures without him, my life never really at a standstill, but I always kept him in the back of my mind, and every now and then, he would call or send me an e-mail. In turn, I'd send him some of my computer art or drop a card in his mailbox and wait for a reply, but often there was none.

What would a guy like him see in someone like me anyway? He could probably have most any woman he wanted.

I talked to Dr. Braunwald about him, along with many other topics, and she tried to advise me. She talked about the stages of development and what men and women expect from each other. When I asked her why men didn't find me more attractive, she said, "You don't have passion."

What in the world did she mean by that? I could be passionate. There had to be something else. What was it that she saw that I couldn't?

I was a misfit like the dentist from *Rudolph the Red Nosed Reindeer*. That's what it was. I was too tall, too smart, my shoulders were too big, my hair was coarse, and I lacked poise and grace. I didn't know how to make myself more attractive. I read all the fashion magazines, and I listened to my friend Pam tell me all about her approach to men, but I was different. How was I to learn about this new body I had?

The first man I kissed was a person whose name I can no longer remember. We had gone to a movie, I believe. When we arrived back home, he awkwardly put his hand on my leg. In response, I turned my head toward him and kissed him. I tried to convince myself that we might make a good pair, but admittedly I found him aloof and at times rather judgmental. He didn't know I was a transwoman at first, but when he eventually found out, it wasn't long before our relationship ended.

I tried dating services and had a few successes but none that lasted more than three or four dates. One guy kissed so badly, I could have drowned from his saliva. My first couple of bedroom trysts were pretty terrible, too. I was caught up in the fantasy of being a woman, and I forgot to think about the fact that penetration might hurt. The take-home message: sex is only fun when your partner is sensitive and caring.

It always seemed the people I found most attractive didn't see me the same way. I so hopelessly lacked confidence in myself. I wanted so much to be in a relationship with a man while playing the role of a woman that I was willing to settle for someone whom I had little in common with. None of those first few dates I had with men were very amorous. I guess there's some truth to the saying, "You have to kiss a lot of frogs before you find a prince."

Dr. Braunwald tried to help me, but she couldn't possibly understand my life fully. She could never really know my heartaches, only her own. I tried to communicate my feelings, but she didn't know how to help me. She knew how to guide me through the early parts of my transition, the discovery phase and the preadolescent stage, but she didn't know how to help me once I was no longer a child. No one did.

I took refuge in my work and dedicated my spare time to my creative talents, dance and writing mainly. When I felt there was no one there to console me, I had Abby.

Realizing I Had Support

Of all the things I hate, I hate being alone the most. I panic and become frozen in a sea of thoughts. It's as if the world might come to an end at any minute. It's an emptiness as difficult to dismiss as knowing you're going to die someday. I have friends I can call and places I can go, but when I feel this way, I just want someone to hold me and tell me they love me.

I hate wasting time, too. Television bores me, unless it's a movie I really want to see. I need distractions, mountains to climb, obstacles to overcome, and problems to solve. I need to learn new things all of the time. It's not enough for me to be part of the status quo. I always feel like I need to prove myself. Is that a good or bad thing? I don't know. Maybe it's both.

I first met Meredith as a patient some ten or more years ago. I believe nothing ever happens by chance. I went through some rough years after coming out at work. When I changed practice locations, Meredith sought me out as a friend. While I struggled to maintain my dignity and self-worth in the community, she and her family welcomed me into their home. They didn't care that I was changing my sex. That was never the main topic of conversation. They had faith in me, and they gave me the strength to persevere.

Over time, our friendship grew. Not to write about it would be an injustice. Meredith loved to entertain, and cooking was her specialty. A master chef would have a tough time competing with her. More importantly, I could talk to her about pretty much anything.

"I've had such a crazy life, Meredith. Do you think I'm OK? I mean, do I have a mental illness?"

She replied, "You're not crazy. You are who you are. You're a good person and you're a good doctor and you're my friend."

"Do you think God loves me? I mean, sometimes I think I'm here for a purpose and I'm supposed to do something, but I don't quite know what it is I'm supposed to do. It's weird. It's like I live for some higher power."

"I don't know. I try not to think too much about things like that. You're just here, and then you die. You've got to make the best of what you have. That's what I think," she said empathetically.

Meredith's loyalty to her friends was surpassed only by her generosity. On a holiday, it wasn't unusual for her to host twenty or thirty people at her home for dinner.

She was born and raised in South Boston, and her use of the English language was often atrocious. I joked with her about that, but she was always thoughtful.

One year, when I was feeling a little down, she threw me a surprise birthday party. It's hard to forget people who do things like that for you. Not only were all of her family there, but my parents, my aunt, my kids, and even Pam showed up. We had an outdoor barbeque, balloons and streamers decorated the yard, she made a beautiful cake for me, and I got some wonderful presents.

She was a waitress when she was younger, and she knew all of the trade workers—the best electrician, the best carpenter, the best person to give you a good deal on a car, and who might best be able to get you out of a traffic ticket. She was street smart, and she knew how to get things done.

My skills were more abstract. I was more computer-savvy, and memorizing strings of numbers or words came easy to me. I also knew how to work through problems without letting my emotions blindside me. Although I had an artistic side, the left side of my brain dominated. Whereas Meredith was a practical person, I was more of a scientist; she liked to stick with what worked for her, and I was more willing to experiment with new ideas. We both used our intuition to solve problems, but I was less trusting of other people than she was. Together, we complemented each other, and our differences helped us become good friends.

My private life was full of mixed emotions. Too often I would find myself in a funk, and if left alone I'd stare at the walls for hours and fall into a horrible depression. Winter was always the worst. I hated the dark and the cold. Isolation drove me nearly insane. Maybe the depressive episodes were a result of divorce, the hormones I was taking, or just getting old. I don't know, but Meredith always tried to support me. She saw the good in me when I could only see my weaknesses.

Work, on the other hand, kept my mind engaged. Trying to understand other people's problems and empathizing with them gave me strength. Physical maladies could be challenging, but that type of problem was fun to solve and generally straightforward. Emotional problems were another story. How could I fix other people when I couldn't fix myself? Sometimes the only thing I could do was listen. It would frustrate me to no end because my traditional medical training was often useless. I didn't have the right tools. People didn't need a pill. That was just a Band-Aid. What they needed was something less tangible, something only they could know. Often what they needed wasn't obvious, and even if they or I figured out what it was, it wasn't always obtainable.

As for me, I struggled constantly with my own emotional problems. Acceptance and rejection by others were on the top of the list. Although I was happy that I could now be true to myself, it saddened me that some people were unwilling to accept the new me. In addition, I couldn't erase from my memory events that happened to me in my childhood, and I couldn't escape the lasting effects they had on me, much as I tried.

Meredith knew when I was troubled, and she had a way of sensing when I wasn't doing well.

"Meredith, I wish there was more money to go around. I feel bad that I can't do more for Jonathan, and I worry about what will happen to Adam when he finishes high school. I shouldn't have bought that dress last week. If I had just stayed the way I was and didn't get divorced, everyone would be better off. The kids would have what they want, Madge wouldn't be worried about having to sell our house, and I wouldn't be living in a mobile home with my job in jeopardy."

"You should stop feeling guilty. You do the best you can for your family. It's the economy. We're in a depression. If you hadn't changed, you would have been horribly unhappy and what kind of father would you have been then? You would have hurt your kids even more, and you would have never have had the chance to be you. You remember that sewing class we took last year? Remember the pants I made that looked like an upside down "U," and remember how we laughed about how they looked like something that was taken off a cowboy after riding his horse? What about your dance classes? What about tap and ballet? Do you think that if you'd stayed Jacob you would've ever discovered your love for dance? If you hadn't changed, you might never have had the chance to experience those things. No, it is what it is, and you've got to let go."

What was the truth? How could I know if I was being honest with myself? Maybe this part of the story would be easier for someone else to write. I had given up a lot financially. Was it fair for others to ask me to give up more? I didn't get to see my kids very often, which was partly my fault, I guess. I didn't fight for custody rights. I didn't have a place for them to sleep. The mobile home was too small for two bedrooms, and the pullout couch was no way for them to share space with me. Besides, they weren't too keen on spending a lot of time with me anyway. Guilt: it always seemed to consume me. Could a different life have made a difference for me? If only I could have been a little girl during my childhood. In many ways I felt like I was making up for lost time, but it came with such a cost.

Coming Into My Own

As time went on, a curious thing started to develop between Calvin and me. Some might call it love, and maybe it was, but there was a bit of an illusion to it at first, as well. For my part, I wanted, in essence, to be a real woman, so I was careful not to reveal much of my past to Calvin. Sure, he had read about me in the newspapers and on the Internet, but just as Madge and I pretended for so many years that there wasn't another side to me, so, too, did Calvin and I. When I was with him, I focused on the fantasy, rarely bringing up anything that might suggest I was once someone else. With time, the fantasy I envisioned and projected outward became my reality: I was his girlfriend. What did our relationship mean to him? I wish I could answer that. Ours was not that of a typical love story; or maybe it was.

It's comical that I don't remember the first night we slept together. It was early October of 2008, and I was about to fly to Rome for a twelve-day cruise of the Mediterranean, Italy mostly. A girlfriend, who worked as a nurse, asked me a year prior if I'd like to go with her. Now, after months of saving and planning, I was about to take the trip that I'd dreamed of all my life.

Calvin and I had already been on a couple of dates together, but it had been a few months since I last saw or heard from him, and I wasn't sure how he felt about me. I was dressed in my nightgown and had just taken something to help me fall asleep when the phone rang.

"Hi, Jessica, Calvin here. How are you?"

I was excited to hear his voice. Maybe he is interested in me after all, I thought. "It's good to hear from you. I'm doing OK. I'm getting ready to go on a cruise to Europe in a couple of days…and you? How are you doing?"

"I was thinking of you tonight. Just thought I'd call and talk to you. That's exciting…going to Europe. Have you ever been there before?"

"No, this will be my first time. I'm flying to Rome, where I'm meeting up with a girlfriend, and then from there, we'll be traveling together by ship. We're planning to see the Vatican, the island of Capri, Naples, Florence, Venus, Dubrovnik, and Barcelona. Do you feel like coming over?"

Stop! What had I just said? It was eleven o'clock at night. I felt this rush of trepidation spread from my head down to my toes. Silence. An eternity passed in a moment.

"Well…sure. I'll be right over."

What was I doing? Did I think we'd just get together for small talk? No, I knew what I was doing. I just didn't want to give myself the time to analyze the situation, sort of like jumping into a pool of cold water without first getting your toes wet.

"See you when you get here," I said with a degree of nervousness.

"OK." Click!

I stood holding the phone to my ear while staring at a chest of drawers in my bedroom; my heart fluttered and my breath quickened by the thought of what might happen between us.

Calvin lived just one street over from me in the mobile home park we considered home. It wasn't congested like some parks, and the lots were big, with plenty of trees and bushes. No sidewalks though, but most of the occupants were over fifty, and there was little motor vehicle traffic late at night. It would take Calvin less than ten minutes to walk to my house from his.

A knock at the door and I knew it was him. What would I say?

"Just invite him in," I said to myself. I turned the knob and opened the door.

"Hi, Jessica. Thanks for inviting me over. Nice to see you."

I wasn't sure what to say; my attraction to him was always amplified by his presence. With the door half open between my porch and the living room, the light from inside helped silhouette his shape while he stood forefront in the shadows. He was smiling, and I wondered what he was thinking. Was he as taken by me as I by him?

"Hi. Come on in," I said, pretending as if I knew how a girl should present herself in such a situation.

He had a rugged manly look, and I sensed he knew when a woman was vulnerable. I smiled and felt an energy drawing me toward him. He reached out his hand gently, as if to gain my trust, and seeing no deceit in his eyes, I moved closer. I could sense his confidence. So strange, this power a man could have over a woman: primal, instinctual, part of the mating process I surmised. No need to run away; we were matched.

It was then that I realized I was standing there in my nightgown. How inviting. A thrill went through me; I subdued my passion, and then gave in to it. I wasn't afraid. He moved closer, and I felt my space combining with his, as if two bubbles floated in the air and joined together.

His scent was alluring, comforting like a flannel shirt in winter. He leaned his head forward to kiss me while he slowly led my hand down by my side, his fingertips touching mine, as if asking for my submission. Willingly, I complied.

His lips were now pressed against mine as I tilted my head backward and gently to one side, eyes closed, my other hand placed gently on his shoulder, my right heel lifted off the floor, exploring every aspect of his mouth.

"Oh, Jessica, you don't know what you do to me."

I grinned. It was time for me to be the seductress. I squeezed his hand and leaned into him for another kiss, this one more fervent than the first. I wrapped my arms lightly around his neck, capturing him while giving him the illusion that my grasp was weak and that he could easily escape me.

He embraced me, kissing me, turning me, moving me backward into the bedroom. I resisted little, fell onto my bed, recovered, pulled the blankets over me to hide my innocence, and waited while he quickly undressed to his underwear and slid in next to me.

Quivering, I hoped kissing him would ease my anxiety. It did. His body was warm, and even though I was scared, I felt wonderfully alive.

"I can play some music if you like? Is it OK if I turn off the light?"

I had an alarm clock/CD player next to my bed, and I often would play soft music while drifting off to sleep. Even with the light extinguished, the room was not completely dark; moonlight shone through a large window to the side of my bed, and the face of the alarm clock was illuminated by blue light. Debussy's "A Little Night Music" was already in the player. Clumsily, I reached over and turned it on.

As I lay back down, he took hold of my hand. As if leading me across a great divide, he made me feel safe. I gazed up at the ceiling, listening attentively to the sound of his breath, fearful to move, fearful of my own desires. Placing my hand on his thigh, I contemplated what I should do next.

"Do what seems natural, Jessica. Let go! Let go!" said a voice in my head. "You're free. Be who you want to be."

Dreamlike, I remember the touch of his skin, the beating of his heart, the sense of bliss that overtook me. Further details one can only imagine, for the sleeping pill I had taken earlier in the night was starting to take its effect.

Are men and women really that different? A force we refer to as lust helps drive reproduction. We all know that, but we seem keen to take sides. Nature, however, cares little what part you play in the process, as long as the species is able to propagate. This was my lesson to learn.

The next morning, still sleepy, I remember watching Calvin get dressed. He had to go to work. Before leaving, he leaned over to kiss me good-bye. He had a smile on his face, and somehow I knew everything between us had been good.

FEELING ESTRANGED

Time has a way of stretching itself out and contracting itself in like a rubber band, yet its relevance is only important to our senses. Take the morning sun and the quietness of the trees ushering in another day. What defines this point in time? We see the brightness of the blue sky, feel a gust of wind against our cheek, smell the fragrance of fresh grass, and hear the buzzing of a bee; each event is separate to our individual senses, but together they form a moment.

It was quiet in the waiting room of Dr. Braunwald's office, and a stillness seemed settled in the air. All that could be heard, other than the deep exhalation of my breath and the chattering of my teeth, was the occasional sound of the wind chime located just outside the entranceway. The furniture was not new but functional and comfortable. The office space was actually a renovated basement in the lower part of her home, and the waiting area appeared to have once been a ground-level porch with one half sectioned off and encompassed by a couch, a few chairs, and a coffee table. There was a pegboard with pushpins near the entrance door holding up various pamphlets and notices and a bookcase below it. A framed document titled *Mental Health Bill of Rights* hung to the left of the pegboard. Lastly, there was an odd square object near a windowsill with mysterious black-and-red wires extending down from it, and there were pictures of horses and a framed silhouette of an African woman further decorating the walls.

I let my eyes close and thought about what might soon transpire. Typically I wrote down a list of items I wanted to discuss, but today there was no need for that. My hands started to shake, and my pulse began to quicken. I knew that shortly Dr. Braunwald would come out to escort me back to her office. I looked around and tried to imagine what connection each object in the room had to one another. A lifetime of memories was presented here, but their origin and deeper meaning would never be revealed to me, as I was simply a patient, and these treasures, recollections of her past, were not meant for me.

Time had a way of being both my friend and an adversary. I had so many things I wanted to talk with her about, but my visits always seemed to end too soon, and the next always seem an eternity away. I stared at the bookcase in front of me. The volumes it contained never appeared to move or change positions from one month to the next. I wished I had time to read every one of them. Maybe then I could leave the fish bowl I envisioned myself in and move past the barrier that separated her world from mine.

Why did this matter so much? What continued to draw me here? What had Dr. Braunwald become to me? I had resisted seeing a psychologist when Dr. Gransby first recommended it. Now I wanted to come here all of the time. Was it a maternal relationship? We weren't that different in age, although she was a little older than me. Why did I want her to take on that role? Oddly, what she possessed and I needed most, she couldn't give me. Her profession prohibited it. She was more like my own mother than I think she realized; neither women were able to show me any affection.

She had qualities I admired though, like an appreciation for art, spirituality, and an open mind. She liked horseback riding, and she was educated. My own mother possessed none of these attributes. How could I find a way to connect with her and open a path to her heart? I wasn't looking for physical love, just some clue that my pursuit of her acceptance was acknowledged. It was that hopeful glimpse of approval, never outwardly attainable, that kept me coming back.

She stepped out of her office and headed down the hallway toward me. I pretended not to look or let her know I was anxious for her arrival. "Jessie, do you want to come back?"

The hallway was long and narrow, and there was always some confusion as to who should enter the room first. The office, like the waiting area, had a comfortable couch, but this room seemed more inviting. The lighting was more subdued and intimate. There was a desk, located in a far corner, with a window in front of it, allowing a view of the grass and trees in the backyard, with a limited view of the sky. I imagined her in a moment of solitude, dreamlike, contemplating the beauty of nature and her own existence. Four or five model horses sat on a small table next to her, and I wondered if she bought them herself or if someone else had given them to her? Based on their different sizes and their individual appearances, I guessed they were acquired at different times, possible while on vacation trips, or as birthday or holiday gifts. We both took our seats, and I contemplated how to begin.

A week earlier, I had lost my job. I had feared it for months, and when administration requested a meeting, I knew something bad was likely to happen. When I arrived, a company executive handed me an envelope containing my employment termination papers. I was devastated, but in reality, my employer and I had been on a collision course for a few years.

I was frightened. How would I survive? I had been trying for over a year to find another job that would be a good fit, but no one was willing to hire me. The initial interviews usually went well, but then a change would occur, and I sensed my past was no longer a secret. I was a physician living in a mobile home, and most of my financial resources had been lost in divorce or used for gender reassignment surgery, facial reconstruction, voice training, electrolysis, new clothes, and other costs related to my transition.

I had e-mailed Dr. Braunwald shortly before this visit, forewarning her of my misfortune, and I was expecting her to ask me to talk about it today. After all, losing one's employment is right up there with the death of a family member, loss of a friend, or some other devastation.

"I'm scared," I told her. "I'm going to be unemployed in a couple of weeks, and I don't know how I'm going to get through this!"

She took a moment to gather her thoughts, and a silence filled the room. The crisis I faced was obvious to both of us, and I waited anxiously for her response. She was trained to be neutral and to avoid expressing her own emotionality. How would I be able to tell if she cared about me? Or was I just another fifty minutes in her day, a twenty dollar co-pay? I couldn't accept the latter, even if it was true. Divorcing, losing my house, my brother, friends, and now my job were nothing compared to the thought of empty exchanges occurring between us. She had to feel something for me!

At times like this, I would often ask myself, "Is there no part of me big enough to affect her? What is her motivation for providing counseling to the transgender population? Is this her way of finding forgiveness for some previous transgression? Was I here by choice, or did some force summon me here? Was I a messenger, as I sometimes imagined, or just another crazy patient? If it was the former, what message was I supposed to deliver?"

Maybe I could communicate with her through my art, not my ability to draw or paint, but rather my ability to move words on a piece of paper. I wanted to convey the message to her that no matter how difficult life could become, I was determined to survive. Where did that strength come from? It came from her. Maybe that was the message I needed to deliver.

I brought this story with me and handed it to her, only not the completed version because that ending was still unknown. She didn't want to read it at first and tucked it under a book, giving me the look that suggested frustration with my attachment to her.

"Let's talk about you. What are you going to do now that you've lost your job?"

"I'm going to start my own practice," I replied. "What other choice do I have?"

"Well, tell me what happened!"

I really wished we could talk about anything else, but I knew if I didn't oblige her, she wouldn't agree to talk to me about what I felt really mattered; how important I felt she was to my overall well-being. I showed her my business plan that was in development and some of the properties I was looking at for office space. I wanted to reassure her that I wasn't giving up, but I also wanted to let her know this might be the last time I'd see her for a while. Like a child craving affection, I wanted her to be proud of me, to place me on a pinnacle and say, "This is my creation. See how wonderful she is!" But she couldn't. My heart ached. Would I be forever unable to change my fate, powerless to avoid the maternal emptiness of my male self?

"Will you read my story?" I asked. "I think it will help."

"Help with what? I'm not going to read it now!" She scowled.

I thought back to some of our first encounters and recalled the excitement I felt in learning that my female gender identity was not a perverse expression of poor mental health but rather a manifestation of a brain that was wired female and trapped in a male body. I had a whole new life to explore, one that was of my choosing, and one that she played a large part in developing. Back then I expected her to share in my joy, but I often sensed apathy instead. I had failed to realize that what I considered a revelation, she had seen many times before. I was not unique, just financially advantaged.

I thought back to all of the times I had disappointed her. Shortly after reading *True Selves*, a book she recommended, I wanted to tell everyone in the world that I was transgendered and say to them all, "Hey, I'm really a girl." But that was a bad idea, and she knew it. People associate a certain image with the person you present to them, and when you replace that image with one that is foreign, they see the falsehood and feel betrayed. The change needs to be gradual so they can adjust. I was too selfish to understand that back then. Like a racehorse already halfway around the track and the gate still open, there was no stopping me. Frustrated by my callous behavior, she e-mailed me and wrote, "You need to slow down and give people time to get used to the changes occurring in you. You need to tell one or two people a month and not one every other day!" Then somewhat sarcastically, she added, "Or you can buy a hundred copies of *True Selves* and give one out to each of them!"

When I discussed plans to come out at work with only one ear pierced and my eyebrows still thick and unruly, she scolded me. Although her aim was likely to protect me from social humiliation, I think I would have preferred that she pretend not to see my lack of feminine grace and instead provide me with guided encouragement, as an elder might do with a small child.

I was saddened when she refused and then delayed writing a letter for me supporting gender reassignment surgery for six months. When she suggested that if I disagreed with her recommendation, I could find another therapist, I felt hurt, not by her decision but rather by her suggestion of abandonment.

Many a visit, I seemed to fail her, but I kept trying. I bought pizza and soda one night for her support group, even though I was unable to attend. I wanted her and everyone in the group to like me and to appreciate my generosity, but she proved reticent to give me credit for my intentions. I gave her cards and small gifts, experiencing great joy when she would accept them, and heartfelt disappointment when she refused.

When I learned that her birthday was in January, I conceived a plan to give her a gift of anonymous theater tickets. I was hoping that by giving her something of this magnitude, and not requesting acknowledgement, I'd somehow prove to myself that my feelings were genuine. I placed them in a box, wrapped it with pretty paper, and hand-tied the bow. I enclosed a card with a typed note pasted inside, so she wouldn't recognize my handwriting, and packaged it for mailing with the address label typed as well.

Sadly, my plan turned into a disaster. She knew it was from me and chided me for my behavior, remarking that if I didn't take the gift back, she would no longer see me. What was I thinking? How could I have deceived myself into believing she wouldn't recognize the sender! I cried all the way home that day.

Nothing I did seemed to be enough. I could no more please her than I could my own mother. Ironically, the more she adhered to the role of the therapist, the more I felt rejected.

Then one day, during a typical visit with her, she remarked that I had a "narcissistic wound."

"What's that?" I replied. "I'm not narcissistic! That's a person who loves him or herself. I'm not like that...am I?"

I took a minute to reflect and then added, "I always try to think of others, and I try to do nice things for people. I'm full of fault and not afraid to admit it, and I try to be respectful of other people's differences. Why would you say I'm narcissistic?"

She tried to explain. "People with a narcissistic wound are always looking for external validation and approval. The wound is said to come from a sense of not feeling loved or being worthy by others. Didn't you once say your mother treated you harshly as a child?"

I became lost in thought, scanning all of my memories, looking for any evidence to support her theory. Child abuse, all those whippings, being born with a genital deformity, always feeling different, other kids making fun of me, the scan stopped there, and the screen froze. Nothing could be heard but static.

The narcissistic wound is sometimes referred to as the "emptiness wound." That's what I learned after leaving her office and researching the term on the Internet. How could I heal from that? Was it even possible? I decided to do some additional reading and learned of Alice Miller, a writer who has written extensively on this subject. Based on her advice, I tried to write a letter to the little boy I once was, acting as his enlightened witness. It helped some.

Dear Jake,

I know you don't know me yet, but I know you very well. I know everything about you, and I know how much you have suffered. Someday you will do great things. For now, you need to know that the deformity you were born with is going to cripple you and cause you great embarrassment, but you aren't inferior to the other boys. You have many great qualities that make up for your shortcoming, such as your love for animals and your ability to learn new things. You're a very bright little boy. I read your poem "Balloons" that got published in the Recorder. *It was very well written.*

I know you love your dad very much, and you wouldn't do anything to ever hurt him. I recall one time you walked with him to the penny candy store holding his hand, and he brought you there just to be with you. Then there was the time he bought an old bicycle for you when you were five and painted it like new and put blocks on the pedals so you could ride it. You like to jump the waves at the ocean with him. He likes to play catch and basketball with you in the driveway. He showed you how to throw a horseshoe. You had a lot of fun with him shooting old TV tubes with a BB gun, and there was that time you played craps with him, and he kept saying, "Double or nothing," until you won his whole paycheck. Of course, he couldn't give you all that money, but you didn't care. You just thought it was funny that his lesson about gambling backfired.

I know, too, how mean your mother has been to you and how she never holds you or asks you how you're feeling. You may have done some things wrong, but no one deserves to be hit like that. I saw you trying to run from her as she kept hitting you, and then she got you cornered in the bedroom and whipped you until there were welts on your back and legs. I know it must have been very painful, and I know it has happened many times. I want to hug and hold you. You can cry, and I will comfort you. I will wipe away your tears. You don't need to be forgiven, because nothing you did was so horrible that it required this kind of punishment. The fact that you endured such cruelty is a testament to your strength and courage. You are truly a wonderful boy who deserves to be loved.

I know it's hard for you to understand that what I'm saying to you now is true, but some day you will learn the truth, and you will remember this letter and the fact that I am always with you.

Love,
Jessie

That little boy, the one inside me, just wanted someone to hold him and tell him he was OK. If only Dr. Braunwald could understand that.

I begged her to read my story, or at least as much as I had written at the time. She finally gave in and pulled it out from under the book that was resting on top of it. Giving me a look of discontent, she snapped, "Did you script this visit?" She began reading it quickly, and I watched her eyes dart back and forth across the page. She eyed me suspiciously, as if looking for some clue to an underlying plan. "I don't get it. What are you trying to say?"

I didn't have a good answer for her. I wasn't sure. What was it that I wanted to say? I took a moment to put together a response.

"I like you and wish I could know you better, but that's not possible, and it hurts. This is the only place where I can talk to you, and you won't ever tell me anything about yourself."

"I'm your therapist. That's the way it's supposed to be!"

She was right, of course, but it didn't take away my pain. I hated being a patient, and yet that's what I was—a transsexual, a person with a gender identity disorder—and every day I had to face the realities of my condition, and I couldn't pretend to be anything else.

How sad I felt. It was here that I learned how to find my "true self," and it was here that I allowed her to study me, to explore my psyche, and postulate theories about my behavior. I had given so much of myself to her. How cruel it seemed that there was no way she could give something back to me. "Maybe in another life," I thought, "I'll be the therapist and she the patient! Wouldn't that be something? Maybe we all have to live each other's lives." How strange my brain works sometimes.

But now forced by circumstances, I had to tell her that I didn't know when I could come back and see her again. Would she care? Would she be sitting at her desk looking out the window someday and think of me? It's not likely that I would ever know. As the visit ended, she shook my hand, and I accepted the gesture, small as it was, and I continued to try to make sense of my life.

What made her special? Why did I admire her so? What prevented me from letting go? Just as Dr. Frankenstein had created the monster that followed him to the edge of the Earth, I, too, yearned to know the person who gave me life. Before the year 2005, I was just a thought, a password on my computer. Now I had a history, and my connection to my former self was just a distant memory.

In the years before my incarnation, Dr. Braunwald had announced to the public her acceptance of people for who they were and stated that she did not judge people by their looks but rather by what motivated their actions. She was an artist, a humanitarian, and a Buddhist. I had fallen in love with her, or whatever she represented to me, but whenever I tried to get close to her, she would appear threatened, and I would need to retreat. When I was alone with my thoughts, I'd think of her, what she might be doing at a particular moment, or whom she might be with, and I would fall into a deep dark well full of sadness. Then I would panic, and my insides would start trembling. Sometimes I could relieve the depression with thoughts of beautiful ballet dancers or some other happy moment, but if I couldn't, I would resort to alcohol or sedatives. My behavior was both irrational and pathologic, but knowing this made it no easier for me to bear.

MAKING IT ON MY OWN

Opening my own practice in January of 2010 was an incredible feat. To say I wasn't frightened to death of failure would be a lie, but Meredith never wavered in her belief in me. From securing a loan, to drawing up a business plan, to gathering and organizing vendor lists, to buying equipment and supplies, to securing insurance contracts, Meredith was there helping me. I was going to hire a lawyer to incorporate myself as a business, but she talked me out of it.

"We don't need to hire a lawyer to do this. We're going to drive to Concord and do this ourselves," she said.

Three hours and $130 later, we were a corporation. We had already secured a lease on some office space, and it was in a perfect location. It was right next to my dance school. Our first task as a new business was to stop at a consignment store and buy a table and chairs. It took two weeks to get phone service installed in the office, so instead we used our cell phones. We sat at that table like it was a command center and made lists of people we needed to call.

"Meredith, how many minutes do you have left on your cell phone?" I asked with cautious optimism, knowing that mine were just about used up.

Each day was like a new battlefront.

"I'll call these insurance companies and see what's going on with our contract status. Can you work on the utilities and get us bottled water? We'll need office furniture, too. I've ordered a couple of computers and a laptop for the office, and I can have the wireless set up by tomorrow," I exclaimed.

"We'll need to go to the hardware store and get sink cabinets, and I'll have my husband Roy plumb the rooms for us. We'll also need someone to tile the exam rooms and carpet the waiting area. I can take care of that."

We were a team, sometimes staying in the office until late in the evening, trying to get the business up and running. We even spent New Year's weekend painting the place with the help of my boys and Meredith's mom. Within a month, the office was open. The Chamber of Commerce even did a ribbon cutting.

The opening was a success, but the weeks and months ahead presented many new challenges. Looking back, it was an adventure.

On the days when we weren't busy, I'd hop in my car, take my cell phone with me, drive around to various nearby establishments, and pass out my business cards. We tried to be inventive. Using a big space in the back of the office, we ran support groups and yoga workshops. We advertised in the newspaper, and I built my own website. In the exam room, rather than the usual display of diplomas, which really said little about a doctor's ability to practice medicine, we displayed pictures of movie stars like Shirley Temple, Judy Garland, and Elvis Presley. In the waiting area, we hung a painting of a beautiful ballerina and another of the Eiffel Tower. We painted the walls a pastel blue, and we had numerous plants in the waiting area to give the office a calming effect.

I practiced traditional medicine in a somewhat untraditional way. I couldn't see twenty-five people a day like many office practices. My patients rarely came to see me with simple problems. Oftentimes their lives were in turmoil, and I tried to do my best to help them. Most days I liked being a physician. It was a challenge, and every time I walked into an exam room, I had a chance to be just a little bit better than the time before. I relied as much on my own experiences as what I had been taught. Learning anatomy and physiology was the easy part.

Helping patients sort through their emotions when they were pre-sented with an illness they didn't expect or understand was the hard part. That took work.

In addition, I've had to accept that I am sometimes powerless to change fate. As a physician, I am never able to prevent death, only prolong its in-evitability. What has intrigued me most about the practice of medicine is that it has a way of continually making me search my soul for the answer to why we exist.

Once, quite a few years ago, I had a patient dying of throat cancer who refused to go on disability right up until a few weeks before his death. He continued to work full-time, even while undergoing chemotherapy. I remember seeing him one morning on rounds in the hospital. He was very upset, pacing back and forth in his room. He had been up most of the night vomiting, and he had not been the kindest to the nursing staff. When I questioned him about the events of the night before, he told me that he was upset because no one would let him see his CT scan. He was an engineer, and he wasn't satisfied in hearing someone's verbal report. He wanted to see the images for himself. I sympathized with him and spoke with the radiolo-gist later in the day. I let my patient know that I made arrangements for a nurse to take him down to radiology where he could sit with the radiolo-gist and view his imaging study, but it couldn't happen until the next day. Unfortunately, he died that night and never got to see those films. I draw some satisfaction from knowing I made the effort and that he knew I did my best to respect his wishes.

On another occasion, as a resident, the nursing staff called me to help with a patient, unknown to me at the time, who was exhibiting violent and threatening behavior. He was throwing furniture and curs-ing at everyone. It turned out that he had been diagnosed with lung cancer, and he was having trouble accepting that he might die soon. I remember taking the elevator up to his room and finding him standing near the bathroom with his IV pole clenched in his hand like a baseball bat and swinging it wildly as three or four nurses tried to calm him down but kept their distance. I don't know what made me feel that I could approach him without harm, but I did. I started asking him ques-tions about his life, not his illness, and once I gained his confidence, we sat down together on the edge of the bed. It turned out that he was the coach of a baseball team, so I talked to him about baseball. I became his friend that night, and I stayed with him for an hour or so. There was no textbook to refer to, only my own ingenuity. He stopped by to see me a few times in the family practice medical center after his hospital discharge. When he saw me, he always had a smile on his face and a degree of optimism for the future. He wasn't ready to give up. I like to think that something I said to him gave him courage.

Over the years, I've learned that determining the best solution to a problem almost always involves first analyzing all of the available information and then taking the time to envision all of the possible outcomes.

For example, a patient who I had been seeing for a few years in the office had been placed in a nursing home because his kidneys were failing and he could no longer take care of himself. I went to see him there one day, not because of any emotional attachment, but rather because Medicare required that I see patients in the nursing home every sixty days. I didn't realize that it was his birthday or that he would die before I ever got to see him again.

In later years, his wife, who was also a patient of mine, would often say to me, "I miss Ronald very much, and it was so nice of you to visit him on his birthday. He thought very highly of you, you know."

The first time she said that to me, I was caught a little bit off guard, because I surmised that she didn't know my true intentions that day. I could've told her what really happened, but I reasoned that telling her the truth would be a mistake. It was better to let her imagine that other people loved her husband as much as she did.

You might ask at this point, do I have any stories of transgendered patients that I'd like to share? Well, the first transgendered patient I ever met was also the patient who inspired me to make changes for myself. He was tall and had little body hair. He related having a lot of difficulty with academics in school as a child. At some point, we did a testosterone level, and it was low. When I tested his chromosome pattern, it turned out that he had a condition called Klinefelter's syndrome. He had an extra X chromosome. Rather than being XY, like most men, he was XXY. I didn't know how he'd take the news and thought he'd be upset, since two X chromosomes are associated with being female, but as it turned out, he seemed gratified to hear the results.

"That explains it!" he said. "That's why I've always felt different."

He wasn't quite ready to tell me what he was thinking, so I left him to contemplate whatever personal meaning the test results had for him, scheduled a follow-up appointment, and moved on to other things I needed to do that day.

A few months later, I learned that he was seeing an endocrinologist and was taking estrogen. "Was that possible? Could I do something like that?" I thought. The specialist he was seeing seemed to be supportive of his decision.

At the time, I tried to put the idea out of my mind. I had a family. I was a doctor, and I had a reputation to uphold. Still, I was intrigued by the thought that a person could change their sex without being a celebrity or a movie star.

Things always seem to happen for a reason. Helping patients come to terms with death has helped me learn compassion. If I hadn't met the gentleman with Klinefelter's syndrome, I might never have had the chance to find my own true self.

I've learned great things from my patients, and being a physician has definitely enriched my life. I feel privileged knowing that people are willing to share their lives with me, but this can also make me feel sad at times because I don't always feel worthy of their respect. There's a part of me that never feels good enough, and I suspect this may be related to childhood trauma. I don't know, but I can't seem to fix it.

The glory of living is recognizing the beauty that lies within each of us. We are all on a journey, and we all have a story to tell.

I wonder sometimes how I would've gotten through my transition without Meredith. She was my saving grace. Many of the transgendered individuals I know aren't nearly as lucky as me. Some have family and friends who refuse to accept them, many have trouble staying employed, and some suffer from serious mental health problems. As a group, they are often misunderstood by society, but individually many of them are wonderful people. As part of that minority, I can't help but feel their pain. I hope someday we will all possess the spirit of forgiveness and tolerance, for it is a virtue that is as much learned as it is a gift.

THE CHOICE

I was alone except for my dog Abby. Meredith had left for home, and I was supposed to finish my work, close up, and meet her later for dinner. There's no way she could have anticipated what I was about to do. She couldn't have possibly known the irrational state of mind I was in. I loved Dr. Braunwald. For going on five years, I had been telling her all of my intimate thoughts and feelings, trusting in her advice but always finding it difficult to gain her approval. I would have given the world for her full acceptance of me.

I sat motionless and zombielike as my heart fell into the deepest, darkest pit you could imagine. It was an effort to breathe, and I could barely find the energy to move my legs.

I checked to see if Abby had adequate food and water, attached her leash, and took her for a walk around the building. While we walked, my heart sank deeper and deeper until it felt like there was no further distance for it to fall. We came back inside, and all I wanted to do was die.

I sat for a moment and contemplated my fate. Then, as destiny would have it, I recalled there was Bosomin in our medication sample closet. I went to it, opened the door, and saw a box of them on the shelf. They were little blue pills, each individually wrapped. I grabbed a handful, stepped back into the hallway, poured myself a cup of water from the bubbler, and sat down at my desk. I laid them all out in front of me, then picked one up and pushed it through its wrapper. I held it in my fingers for a minute, and proceeded to put it in my mouth. I took a gulp of water and swallowed it.

I had taken two before with no ill effect, so I knew I had to take more than that. I pushed another one through its wrapper and held it out in front of me. "Quickly," I thought to myself, "swallow another one. You can do it." I placed it in my mouth and took another gulp of water. "You're almost there. Take another one. You can do it," a voice in my head kept saying.

I loved her. How could she hurt me so? I was born in her office. When I had a problem, I always went to her for help. She had been there with me from the beginning, nurturing my development, but no matter what I tried to do to please her, it never seemed enough. She was at times authoritative, and she often scolded me, yet I still admired her and sometimes wished she had been my real mother. I wanted so much to communicate with that part of her that was unknown to me.

She loved horses. I knew this because of the paintings in her waiting room and the miniatures that sat on an end table next to her. I once took a riding lesson simply because I thought it might provide me with some insight into what she found so special about them. When I shared this with her and commented that she might like to arrange a lesson for herself with the stable owner, she replied rather abruptly, "I have a stable to ride at. I don't need to go anywhere else."

She was a Buddhist. She told me that. But had she always been a Buddhist? What traumas had she experienced in her life? Why couldn't she share any of that with me? All I knew of her private life was what I could read about on the Internet. Her website was called *Art for the Soul*. I loved her art. Her collages were beautiful.

In my mind, I had to go through puberty twice. My first mother had failed to show me any affection as a child, and now my second was doing the same. I had been granted a second chance at life, and yet I couldn't prevent the same sorrows from happening.

At one of our last visits together, she told me that I didn't need to see her anymore and suggested that I used trickery to engage in conversation with her. I always needed her but now more than ever. I had lost my job just a couple of months before, and I was struggling to open my own business. I felt alone, and I was scared.

I stared at the pills on my desk. "Think of them as candy. Take one more. What have you got to live for anyway?"

I have such a dual personality sometimes. I can ride the waves one minute, get my name in newspapers, speak at conferences, write a policy resolution for the American Academy of Family Practice, and so on, and the next minute I feel worthless and lack self-confidence.

Just two nights earlier, Dr. Braunwald's transgender support group met. The group always gathered the first Tuesday of the month, my ballet night. On this particular evening, she planned to do something with the group she had never done before. She announced by e-mail that she was going to do guided imagery. I wanted so much to do this with her, but I also wanted to be with my friends at ballet class. I agonized all day over what I should do. I decided to send her an e-mail explaining my dilemma. I hoped she would help me choose. Right up until ten minutes before the start of my ballet class, I waited for her reply. Finally, with no approval forthcoming, I gathered up my ballet shoes and headed over to the dance studio.

The next day I felt sad and somewhat guilty over the choice I had made. In actuality, I never really needed to ask her for permission to go to the group. I had already been granted that when she included me in her original invitation. Dance had become everything to me, and deep down I knew my place that night was with my friends and fellow dancers. Her group session would have cost me forty dollars, and I didn't really relate to the folks there anymore. Many of them were still in the discovery phase of their transition. The fact that I didn't go suggests what I really wanted from her was affirmation that she understood.

I was no longer a little girl. I was exploring my own interests and finding new ways to express myself. I was like a teenager leaving for college, a daughter giving herself to someone in marriage, or a young girl discovering that she is pregnant. These are all milestones in a woman's life. It was time for me to find my own way in the world. I didn't need Dr. Braunwald anymore, and yet I still did. Just as my real mother rarely displayed affection toward me growing up, neither did Dr. Braunwald. I could only imagine that she cared about me.

I e-mailed her again to tell her how difficult my decision had been. I wanted her to know that I loved her, not as a man loves a woman, but rather as a student admires a teacher or a daughter her parent. I needed her approval, and I wanted to hear her say, "I'm happy for you. I know it's hard for you to leave me, but it's time. I will always be with you in spirit. You can still call on me from time to time, and I wish you the best in your new life. Go forth and make me proud of you."

She wrote back, "If you persist in writing to me like this, I will have to block your e-mail."

I swallowed another pill, and knowing that I would soon be falling asleep, I typed what I thought would be my last message to her.

I wish you could know me. I just want someone to talk to whom I can confide in about my innermost secrets. I took some Bosomin. I don't know when it will start taking effect. I'm a little scared. I've got to take a couple more before I fall asleep. If only you didn't reject me so. If you'd just said you didn't get my e-mail in time or you were sorry. I always looked forward to talking with you because I could tell you things that I'd never told anybody before. I just wanted a friend I could confide in. I can't tell my regular friends the things I talk about with you. I don't want them to see me sad. Hmmm...I've always been able to talk myself out of this before. I don't think anybody knows where I am. That's good. I wish you could have talked to me about Buddha and drumming and horses and what you did in college. You went to school in Texas. Is that where you learned to ride horses? When you were a little girl, did you live in Concord? Greenfield was a small town. We had a river that we all swam in, and I took swimming lessons there in the summer. My friend Tim and I used to float down that river on inner tubes. Meredith is not going to be too happy with me. I just want to keep writing until I'm almost asleep and tell you everything I can think of that I'd like to say. Flowers are pretty this time of year. I wonder what it would have been like to grow up with other girlfriends, have menstrual periods, get pregnant, all that stuff. Do you have any brothers or sisters? Where did you go for vacations when you were a little girl? Were you always a Unitarian? I wish I were pretty. I thought these pills would start working by now. We used to go to Hampton beach when we were kids. I always had a lot of fun with my dad. You know, just writing all these things down and knowing that if I'm dead you can't fire me, makes it a little less anxiety provoking. I attached the picture I wanted to give you. I do believe that there's some purpose for us here on earth. I just read boring medical journals. I wish I could read some of the stuff you read. What was your favorite subject in school? Did you like English? I think if I knew you back then, I would have tried to be your friend. I was always one of the smart kids. You know what's great about ballet? It's the discipline and the fact that I have no inherent abilities for it that makes me like it. I just can't make my body do the right thing, but I also can't give up. What is guided imagery like? I was trying to find information about it online last night. Did you read the dialogue or did you have a tape for people to listen to? Meditation is good. I used to love skipping rope with girls in grammar school until the other boys made fun of it. If I have any books or anything you want, you're welcome to take them. I have over one hundred Eastern Press books with nice binders and gold ribbons, all the classics. I would buy them, one a month, for years. In my T Rowe account, I think I have you getting 10 percent. That'll be good for you and your husband to take a nice vacation with. Take a trip to Europe. Well, I just have a couple more pills to go.

I can feel myself starting to get tired. This isn't such a bad way to go. I've got one more Bosomin tab I should take, and then maybe I'll go lay down with Abby. Tell everybody I fought a hard fight but lost. You win some and you lose some.

Jessie

What happened after that is only a partial memory to me, as I quickly fell into a stupor. I remember going to the refrigerator and finding a jar of olives, only to discover later that I ate every one of them. I remember hearing someone pounding on the door. It was Meredith and her mother. A policeman arrived soon after. I remember hearing voices and someone talking on the phone in the next room. (It was Meredith talking to Dr. Braunwald). I could hear the ambulance crew talking, and a female attendant tried to reassure me that I was safe. I felt her place an IV in my arm, and I could feel the cold crystalloid fluid entering my body.

Madge stayed with me in the emergency room that night. I don't know how she got there or when she went home, but I remember her being by my side. I hurt her more than anyone else, and yet she was still there for me when I needed her.

As morning came, I found myself alone in a small room. A mental health worker came in to talk to me and suggested that I voluntarily admit myself to the hospital. If I refused, she would likely push for involuntary admission because of concerns that I might further hurt myself. Knowing the legal ramifications of this, I agreed to stay.

Soon after, I was transported to a locked-door mental health facility. It was strange to find myself there. I felt like I was at summer camp, only not quite. A nice lady escorted me to a room where there were bins of old clothing.

"You won't want to wear that dress and those high heels here. Let's see if we can find you something to wear. Here, this looks like it might fit you." She handed me a short-sleeve, green, V-neck blouse and a pair of brown pants. "You'll need a toothbrush and some toothpaste, too. Which color would you like, red or purple?"

The mental health unit was all on one floor. It was built as a large square with individual rooms around its perimeter and a separate room in the center with male and female showers. The rest of the floor plan was open. A telephone was attached to one wall of the inner room. To one side of the square, there were two long tables lined up lengthwise, and this is where we ate our meals and sat for group sessions.

In the middle of the open area was a couch, two chairs, and a television set. At one corner, there was a medication room; this is where the staff gathered and worked. A split door guarded the entrance, and the bottom half was always locked. The walls were like those of an old factory. Each person had his or her own room. The beds were made with a single sheet and a blanket. If your shoes had laces, they had to be removed. My personal items, including my wallet, were taken from me and secured in a safe place.

In my youth, I used to go to a place called Camp Anderson in the summer months. It was an overnight camp, and I usually went for two weeks in July. At night, after supper, we would gather near the camp store and watch the counselors play volleyball. Our parents allotted a small amount of money for us to spend at the store, and we could buy penny candy, ice cream, and soda.

The medication room at the mental health unit reminded me of that general store. The employees recognized your face and sometimes knew your name, but they had no vested interest in getting to know you personally. You were just a camper, another patient on the floor. I can imagine prisons and concentration camps with a similar hierarchy. There are those people who are inside, and there are those who are outside, but who is good and who is bad is simply a matter of who has the privilege of being able to leave.

I quickly learned that the only way I was going to get out of there was by participating in the daily group sessions and activities. I never mentioned that I was a doctor to any of the other patients. If I had, they likely would have related to me differently. I didn't want to be different. Although boredom was common, there was a certain amount of camaraderie amongst everyone. I liked that. We were all there because we had made a similar mistake. Those who had already been there for a few days, acted as mentors for those who were new. We all had a story to tell. Although we often shared phone numbers and addresses, I never heard from any of them again after my release.

After three days, they decided to let me go home. The saddest part about leaving was calling Dr. Braunwald and learning that she would no longer see me as a patient. I was devastated, but somehow I knew that would be her response. What I did was wrong, and atonement wouldn't come easy.

GRIEVING MY LOSS

Over the next year, I grieved, and some days were worse than others. Keeping my mind busy seemed to help, but sometimes that feeling of emptiness would catch hold of me, like a big gust of wind that comes out of nowhere, and it would just suck the air right out of me. The rational part of me knew that this made no sense, but there was this other part of me, a part that I've never really been able to understand, that wanted something intangible, something I sensed was not mine to have. It's difficult to describe. I yearn for acceptance, and I want everyone to love me, but I know deep down that's impossible.

I loved Dr. Braunwald, but no matter how much I tried to explain my feelings to her, she seemed to misunderstand my intentions. I admired her and I wanted to hear her say that I was a good person, a decent human being, and that my faults were forgivable. I poured out my heart to her, but her responses always seemed to lack empathy. She couldn't or wouldn't share her emotions with me.

I'd be OK for a few weeks, and then something would trigger that horrible feeling to come over me again. I'd ruminate and talk to myself. I'd say things over and over in my head, or I'd obsess about some thought that might be on my mind. When I was a kid, I remember seeing "crazy" people on the street corner talking to themselves, and now I wondered if I was becoming one of them.

Dance class was the one activity that always lifted my spirits. It had a magical effect on me. It's the one thing that could snap me out of a depression, more than any pill or talk therapy. Who would've ever thought that I'd take a ballet class? No one ever questioned me about my motive for attending. All the other dancers loved it as much as I did. The fact that I was older than most of the other students didn't seem to matter.

After class, when I was generally feeling better, I'd ask myself, "What is it about dance that you like so much?" The answer wasn't obvious. Certainly, being with a bunch of girls having fun together gave me a sense of belonging, but it was more than that. I didn't have to worry about being bullied. As a boy, I lacked the strength and physical prowess of the other boys in my neighborhood. I was accepted amongst them but only as long as I knew my place. I couldn't tell them that I liked playing jump rope with the girls or making cookies with them. I had to pretend I liked football, but I hated it. I didn't like having people knock me down, and I didn't like trying to act tough when I wasn't. It just didn't work for me.

Basketball was one of the few team sports that I liked to play as a boy and later as a young man. I liked playing basketball because it was a game of continual movement, much like dance. You didn't need to be the strongest to play. Agility, coordination, speed, and a sense of timing were just as important. To play well you also needed to know where everyone else was on the court and which direction they might be moving. Much like dance, kinesthetic memory played a key role in one's ability to play the game.

Dance didn't allow my thoughts to stay stuck in any one place. I couldn't let the record in my head play over and over. That's what I did when I was alone, but in dance class it was important to respect the timing and know when to move on to the next step. I couldn't allow myself to hesitate or let myself get bogged down by one mistake. Instead I had to let myself progress with the music, stay with the group, and be part of what was happening around me. That's what I loved about dance. It forced me to experience life, but it let me do so on my terms. I didn't have to worry about anyone pushing or shoving me. It wasn't a contest. I was there enjoying the moment for me, not anyone else.

If only Dr. Braunwald could see the world from my perspective, then she'd understand. I tried to contact her, tried to explain to her what she meant to me, but nothing I said or did made a difference. I had such a powerful attachment to her; it was as if I was under a spell. As much as I tried to let go, I always failed. Strangely, I felt if she could find it in her heart to reach out to me one more time, everything would be OK. I hated the way our relationship ended.

I once saw this cartoon as a kid where a rooster found a baby dinosaur egg and sat on it. When the egg hatched, the baby dinosaur followed the rooster everywhere he went. It bonded with the rooster and thought it was its mother. No matter how much the rooster tried to hide, the dinosaur always found him. Of course, the rooster wasn't his mother and couldn't be anyone's mother but that didn't matter; the baby dinosaur loved him anyway.

My relationship with Dr. Braunwald was something like that. I couldn't find it in my heart to hate her or get angry with her. I dreamed that someday she'd forgive me for feeling the way I did, and she'd take that leap of faith and agree to let me see her once more.

I'm not sure what I wanted to tell her, but certainly I wasn't a child anymore. Maybe I'd tell her that I found the passion she once talked to me about, or maybe I'd tell her that being the girl I always wanted to be was great, but something was still missing. I wanted to hear her say she was proud of me, I wasn't a quitter, my life mattered, and she cared about me. Instead, she refused to acknowledge me or let me communicate with her in any way. I had to learn how to live with that sadness. That was my fate. Nothing ever comes for free, and finding my true self was no exception.

Dancing and Remembering

I stared at the harlequin floor, examining every line and mark on the dulled oak as I tried to memorize the scent of the wood. The piano playing in the background was seductive, and each sound, irresistible, had to be followed to the next as if beckoning me to a place of beauty. I imagined a place where all of the colors were bright, a landscape of trees and meadows, peaceful and sunny, the wind blowing gently, but only when a slight breeze seemed necessary. The music was mine, a gift, and no one could take it from me. As the melody played on, all that mattered was letting myself go, relishing the moment for what it was and trying not to find an explanation for it. I was determined to conquer my inhibitions. If I lacked grace, perseverance would be my strength. I needed to focus my brain to the right and not to the left, train myself to make the movements more fluid and natural.

Maintaining the dream required effort. Thoughts of my past constantly tried to make their way into my consciousness. It was as if an army of old memories refused to be forgotten. "Block them out! Make your mind blank. Don't let them in," I told myself. "Focus! You're a girl. Forget who you once were. Get back to the music. Concentrate! Concentrate!"

"Crack" went the bat. High, high in the air the ball soared, hovering, floating, and then starting its downward trajectory. Fear of dropping the ball consumed me. My dad was watching in the bleachers. Was I going to disappoint him once again? How could anyone catch something so small, travelling so fast, and in such a vast space?

The piano beckoned me back.

"Let the music intoxicate you," I commanded. "Don't let those intrusive thoughts gain hold of you!"

Erin, our instructor, took a moment to demonstrate the steps she wanted us to duplicate and then called them out. "Balancé to the right girls. Now balancé to the left, soutenu, prepare, now pirouette en dehors. Count one, two, three, four...five, six, seven, eight." Her voice was so gentle and pleasing to my ear.

She was short in stature, had red hair, nice cheekbones, and a beautiful smile. Although not small-waisted, she didn't look overweight either. If you looked discernibly, you could see that she had large, powerful calf muscles, probably as a result of years of practice and discipline. She was vibrant, and her enthusiasm for ballet captivated me. Why would I want to be any place but here?

"Does he have to be on my team?" Brian exclaimed.

"I'll take him," said Tim. "He can hike me the ball."

"Good luck! I'm just glad he's not on my team. Do you want to take John and I'll take Keeno just to help make things even?"

Tim was my best friend, and he always looked out for me. I felt protected when I was with him. He was stronger and faster than any of the other kids, and no one dared challenge him. He could throw a football clear across a neighbor's field with a perfect spiral, and if he threw you a pitch, you'd better be prepared as soon as it hit your glove to draw your hand back. Without him, I don't think the other kids in the neighborhood would have let me play with them.

Erin's voice called out to me. "Jessica! Keep your arms rounded on the balancé, pull your tummy in, and keep your hip turned out on the pirouette."

I gave her a nod and a look as if to say, "I can do this with your help. I think you're great."

She walked over and asked me to hold a position in second with a tendu devant; then she began manipulating me like I was a Gumby doll. She started with my fingers, gently moving them so that they looked more relaxed and my middle fingers and thumbs were closer together. Next she put her hands on my shoulders and applied even pressure downward to signal that I needed to avoid contracting them upward. Then she pulled my upper arms out and bent my lower arms in while saying, "You want to be able to have your arms in such a position that a marble can slowly run down your arm." She looked into my eyes and smiled, and I felt special.

Before moving on, she put one hand on the front of my chest and one on my back, squeezed, and pushed forward at the same time. Lastly, with a firm grasp, she grabbed my leg and made sure I was rotated out with my heel presented forward. When she was done, she stepped back to check her work. She looked happy, pleased with my cooperation, and proud of her creation. I cherished times like these. Why couldn't I forget those old childhood memories?

I must have dropped something. Now I was in trouble! I had angered her. I started to tremble and my only thought was to run. Little good it would do me though, as there was no place I could hide and no place to escape. I turned quickly to see how close she was behind me. The rage in her face was that of pure hatred. I scrambled to get up the stairs. She was screaming at me, swinging that thin leather strap just out of reach of me, and calling out my name.

"I'll catch you, you son of a bitch!"

I ran to the bedroom. There was no better choice. I tried jumping from one side of the bed to the other, hoping she might make a mistake and leave me a way out, but it didn't work. She finally got me cornered between the bed and the outside wall, the one near the window. It was sunny outside. As if a moment could last forever, I tried to concentrate on the warm rays that filtered through the glass and the pleasant fragrance of the room, which proclaimed itself my friend and my only witness.

It was time. I let the moment go and prayed that what was to come wouldn't last too long.

The pain was unbearable at first, but then, as I got accustomed to her rhythm, I gained strength in my ability to endure each thrashing. I tried to think of other things. "When will this be over?" I asked myself. "When will she stop?" The welts on my back and legs weren't nearly as painful as her lack of acceptance and her inability to love me.

"OK girls, take a break and get a drink if you need it! Be back in five minutes." Erin took a seat near the amplifier and watched us as we headed out of the room.

The waiting area had a table, a bathroom with a drinking faucet, and about a dozen chairs evenly divided across from each other. I sat down to rest for a minute, and Julianne stepped over next to me.

"Hi, Jessie! How are you? How's your week been? My sister and I are playing in *Luck is Just Around the Corner* next week. It's a musical at the Peterborough Theater. Why don't you come? It should be a great show."

I was glad to have her as a friend. She was a senior in high school, and her parents owned two horses. When she talked about them, she always got giddy. As I looked at her with her hair pulled back, her cheeks puffed and rosy, and her teeth with braces that showed no lack of confidence, I could tell she had never been wounded.

"Really! Maybe I can make it. What part are you playing?" I asked.

"I'm going to be one of the chorus girls," she replied. "My sister is playing the part of Georgette, the Italian sales woman."

"OK girls, Come on back," Erin hollered out to us. "Stretch for a few minutes, and we'll go through the routine again."

Julianne and I turned and walked back into the dance area with the other girls.

I sat down with my back straight, my knees pointing out, and the soles of my feet pressed together. As I started my stretching routine, my mind began to wander.

The ball started its accelerated descent, speeding toward me.

My dad was a kind and gentle man. He spent countless hours playing catch with me in the driveway of our home, always encouraging me. Somehow I knew, though, that I was going to drop it. Maybe if I were lucky, it would at least hit the tip of my glove.

No such luck!

The game wasn't over, but my one chance to make my dad proud of me had happened, and I let him down again.

Later, when we were walking to the car, he put his arm around me and said, "Good game, Jake! You almost got that pop fly. It was pretty high, a tough one for anyone to catch!"

"Girls, let's form three lines of four. I want the first line to do a count of eight, just like we practiced before break, then the second line, do the same, and then the last line."

I looked at myself in the mirror wearing my pretty pink leotard, my flowered skirt with tights, and ballet slippers. My shoulders were broad. I looked taller than the other girls. I didn't move the same as them. As we performed our routine, I seemed always to be a step behind everyone else.

I thought back once more to those days when I was twelve playing Little League. I was on "Rotary." That was the name of our team. My hair was short and slicked up in the front. I wore a gray uniform with dark blue stirrups, white socks, and a blue hat with an "R" on the front. Back then a new baseball glove was the envy of all the other boys in the neighborhood. Once Tim and I each got one around the same time. He had this idea that we could soften the leather pocket with a banana peel, and he talked me into folding my glove over it and sleeping with it under my mattress. I never did find that it made much of a difference. He was a good friend though, and I enjoyed playing catch with him as long as he didn't throw it too hard.

I guess my memories weren't all bad. I miss Tim sometimes and suspect, given all that's happened to me these past few years, he would still stand up for me. That's just the type of person he was. He was able to see things in me that no one else could.

I looked in the mirror again. I was as awkward now as I felt back then. Something was different though, but I couldn't quite put my finger on it. My legs started to tremble, and the left knee I injured while playing basketball many years ago was beginning to ache. I'd been dancing nearly three hours that particular night, and I could barely hold my weight much longer.

Suddenly, tears in my eyes started to well up, not because I was in pain but because I was happy. I loved being there in the dance studio with all of those wonderful girls. I belonged there. I looked up at the clock. It was 9 p.m. Erin signaled to us that class was over, and we made a line, facing forward, to curtsey to the imaginary audience in front of us. We always did this at the end of class. As we each said our good nights to one another, I thought about all of the hardships I had faced and all of the obstacles I had overcome. I waited until everyone had left the room and looked back into the mirror. For a moment, I thought I could hear someone clapping, but then realized it was just the old ceiling fan making an uneven revolution. I curtsied once more then thanked the audience for coming. Maybe my performance wasn't that bad after all.

REUNITING WITH MY BROTHER

I t was springtime in the year 2011, and my birthday was fast approaching. As I sat with my friend Matty in Saint Jude's Church watching my niece's First Communion, I thought about all that had happened to me over the past six years. I didn't consider myself Catholic anymore, but I felt a need to be respectful of the ceremony and all of the people who had gathered there to celebrate the occasion. When it came time for everyone to receive communion, I felt like crying, not because of the sheer spectacle of the event, beautiful as it was, but rather because the overwhelming guilt I had experienced in a church similar to this one when my father-in-law died was no longer there.

Everyone was dressed in his or her Sunday best. The church was already packed when we arrived, so we seated ourselves in the back, barely able to see the children or the altar. The music was nice, although somewhat traditional. I could hear a guitarist accompanying the chorus.

Matty was a transguy, although you'd never know it except for his small size. His heart was as big as an elephant's, and he loved me. If only people knew our story. Who would believe Matty was once a girl and I was once a boy? Doesn't that sound like something from a circus attraction? I wanted so much to love him because we shared this oddity of nature called gender dysphoria, but I could never quite find it in me. He was my friend, and he understood more than anyone else what I had been through, but I often had to tell him, and remind myself, that physical attraction was guided by some sort of Darwinian biochemistry orchestrated to propagate the species, pheromone-driven maybe, but something people likely had no control over. I loved him, but I didn't. He just hated it whenever I told him that.

My brother was sitting on the opposite side of the church from us. I caught a glimpse of him sometime around the middle of the service when everyone stood up to sing. What would I say to him? I was glad he had invited me. He had only recently seen me for the first time as Jessica after a family reunion. Prior to that, we hadn't seen each other since the Christmas of 2004, shortly after the Red Sox won the World Series.

That family reunion, honoring my aunt and uncle's sixtieth wedding anniversary, turned out to be a very emotional event, as I suspected it might. There were dozens of people gathered there, both inside and outside of my cousin's house. While gazing out through the picture window in the living room, I saw my brother and his family arrive. I wasn't sure what to do. How would he react to me being there? After pulling into the driveway and getting out of his car, he walked to the backyard to mingle and converse with the people there. I, in turn, moved to the other side of the house and gazed out the kitchen window at him. He was heavier than I remembered him, and his hair had grayed considerably. How long could we avoid each other, I wondered? The minutes seemed like hours, but I knew our meeting was inevitable.

Then it happened. Someone wanted to get a family photo and asked everyone to gather in the backyard. What was I to do? I was terrified, but I also felt an overwhelming need to reunite with my brother. I waited until almost everyone was standing or sitting in position, and then I moved in next to my parents. I could see my brother out of the corner my eye. I knew he saw me as well. My mom stood between the two of us, and I tried to maintain my gaze forward for the photographer. I knew that when it was over I'd have to confront him.

"Smile everyone," said the photographer as his camera clicked. He took four or five snapshots, and when the shoot was over, I wished I could be anywhere else, but there was no escape and no place to hide. I was standing three feet away from my brother, wearing a dress and sporting a butterfly tattoo on my left upper chest that everyone could clearly see. I felt as if I had deceived him all of my life. How many times when we were younger did I pick on him and try to act as if I was tough simply because I was older? Now I had to show him my true self, and I couldn't help but feel humbled.

I forced myself to turn in his direction, not knowing how he would react. I burst into tears and lunged to hug him. As if not knowing how best to react, he hugged me back. I didn't know what to do after that and quickly moved to the other side of my mother, hoping she might protect me. How ironic! I didn't give my brother much of a chance to talk with me, and I soon found myself back in the kitchen staring through the window at him and keeping my distance. At the end of the day, I said a hasty good-bye.

Many months later, I called my parents one weekend to see if they'd be home, as I was thinking of paying them a visit. My mom answered the phone and told me they would be there, but my brother and his family were planning a visit, too. At first I said, "Maybe I'll come another weekend." But after hanging up the phone, I thought about it and decided that maybe this would be the perfect opportunity for my brother to see me as I really was, the way I wanted him to see me, not as some stereotypical freak but as a real woman who cared about how she looked and how other people perceived her, who was sensitive and beautiful in her own way.

I called back. "Mom, I think I'll come home. Can you save a place for me at the dinner table?"

I decided to dress simply with slacks and a nice top, ballet flats, and my hair pulled back in a ponytail. I arrived at my parents' house before my brother and his family arrived, and when they did, I greeted them at the door. No talk of gender; that was part of my plan. My niece was seven, and she had been taking dance classes for a couple years. I focused my attention on her, and we talked about ballet. There was a commonality between us, and it was that part of me that could relate to her passion, the enchantment of dance, and its ability to express emotionality through movement that I wanted my brother to see.

Later, after dinner, we all drove to the cinema. Unusual as it might seem, after buying our admission tickets and wandering into the darkened theater, we simultaneously came to the realization that we had failed to buy popcorn. My brother, being the gentleman, offered to go get some for us. The rest of us took our seats. My parents sat to my right while my sister-in-law and the children sat to my left. That left one empty seat between my sister-in-law and me. When my brother came back with the popcorn, he had no choice but to sit next to me. I could tell he felt a little uncomfortable, but then so did I. At the end of the night, I hugged him and again we said our good-byes. It was an awkward moment and he looked somewhat dejected, as if someone he trusted had betrayed him.

I have caused so many people anguish. Was it fair for me to have done what I did? I often feel that my destiny is not my own to determine but rather some power rules me and I am simply an agent of change, a messenger, a crusader who fights battles for righteousness. Who is it that I fight for?

I have forced many of my friends to re-analyze their beliefs, and I have caused family to make choices they would otherwise not have had to make. We were all changed in some way, and I feel responsible for much of their heartache, but in reality I am but one node in a vast universe. Changes brought on by my decisions are minuscule in the grand scheme of life.

I have new friends now. Although I will forever carry the memories of old ones with me, it is time to move on and explore the richness of the world before me. I miss John and Eleanor but have long since realized they are not likely to ever be a major part of my life again. I miss Dr. Gransby, too, who lives too far away for me to see her on a frequent basis. For professional reasons, it is probably best she keep some distance from me. I enjoy my one or two visits a year with her as a patient and will never forget that she was the first person I ever opened up to. She will always be close to my heart.

Madge and I do our best to stay friends. I still care about what happens to her, even though we rarely see each other now. It has been over twenty years since we first met, and we are both changed people. We have our children in common, but aside from that our lives move in much different directions.

Jonathan and Adam have moved on with their lives, too. Whereas Jonathan had requested that I not attend his high school graduation and had broken off all contact with me for over a year, we mended our differences some time ago, and we no longer have any animosity toward each other. I see him infrequently, not because of any rift between us but because he lives and goes to school in Boston, and I am busy trying to keep my business going.

Adam lives with Madge, and I see him on weekends. Our favorite thing to do together is to go to the movies. Sometimes I wish I saw him more, but my living arrangements have not always been the most accommodating.

My new friends Pam, Matty, Meredith, and many others, give me strength to face each new day's challenges. I am my own person, a survivor. But my biggest regret is losing Dr. Braunwald. Maybe she felt it was for my own good or maybe she felt I needed to find my own way in the world, but I still miss her. When I started my transition, I never gave much thought to the fact that I would face disappointments. Losing Dr. Braunwald was one of the deepest heartaches of my life. I experienced a grief reaction that was no less severe than if I had lost my biological mother.

Matty has been helpful. I would never have been able to work through my sadness without him. He always seems to understand and lets me talk freely whenever I feel I need to. He gives good advice, but the emotional anguish I feel sometimes is unyielding. No amount of therapy takes it away. I just learn how to live with it better.

Jake still lives deep inside me, and he never really died nor had he gone to sleep. The integration of my male and female selves was now complete, and the epitome of all that was good in me could be expressed without shame.

As Matty and I sat in the church together, I thought to myself, "Does time really heal all wounds? Are we really all here on this Earth for some purpose?"

Everyone stood up by rows and walked to the front to take the Eucharist, symbolic for the body and blood of Christ. I turned and looked at Matty.

"What do you say we take communion?"

RECONCILING WITH MY MOTHER

It was Christmastime 2011 and my parents were planning to stay with me for the weekend. It wasn't actually Christmas day but a few weeks before. Each year my parents alternated between spending Christmas with me versus spending it with my brother and his family. This year I was the odd one out.

I was no longer living in a mobile home. I had bought a detached condominium that was large and spacious with two bedrooms, a sunroom, and a kitchen with a hard wood floor. Now when I had visitors, they no longer had to sleep on a pullout couch.

A few weeks earlier, Matty had helped me put up a Christmas tree at my house. It was just a small one, about four feet high. We decorated it with ballerina figurines and fairies, some colored Christmas tree lights, and a few ornamental bulbs. Matty did most of the work, because I had felt a little bit down that day and had lacked Christmas spirit. The holidays just weren't the same now that my children didn't live with me any longer.

"Jessie, I'm going to cheer you up. I've made homemade pizza and I'm bringing some Christmas movies along with me," he said on the phone just before leaving his house in Keene, New Hampshire, to spend the weekend with me. "I don't like seeing you sad. You've got to think in the present. What happened in the past doesn't matter anymore. If you dwell on it all of the time, the rest of your life will pass you by, and you'll never experience the joys all around you."

He was always so good to me, even asking me to marry him once, but I said no. I couldn't see the point. Marriage in my mind mattered only if you had children or property in common. Besides, I liked him better as a friend.

We had a lot of similar interests. Matty loved ballet as much as I did, and I could listen to him play the piano for hours. He didn't mind watching movies with me that could make a girl cry, going for long bike rides, hiking in the woods, or going shopping with me. When recital time came around, he sat in the audience, cheering me on.

Being a social worker, he knew my grief over the loss of Dr. Braunwald went much deeper than the loss of a person I admired or someone I thought of as a surrogate mother. As much as I knew he was right, no amount of talking with him about it seemed to help. I was stuck as they say. I couldn't get past the traumas of my childhood. They were always in the background like a canvas that had been painted over to make a fresh picture. Sometimes I wished for a machine that could pluck those bad memories from my mind, so I could forever forget them, but there's no such thing. Why couldn't I let go? Why did those memories have to keep haunting me so?

My parents arrived about midday on a Saturday. They brought Christmas gifts to exchange, and I had some to give them as well. When I was small, Christmas was always the best day of the year, and I could barely sleep the night before. Now it didn't hold that same sparkle for me, but perhaps there was still some magic left in it.

I was a little sad that my brother didn't invite me to his house for Christmas this year, but it's possible that he thought I had other plans or maybe he thought that I'd feel awkward. I wasn't going to let that bother me, and I decided to make the best of our holiday get-together.

We greeted each other with hugs and kisses, and after I helped them bring their bags inside, we all relaxed in the living room to the warmth of my gas-lit fireplace. For entertainment, we watched the musical *Annie*. As many of those who've seen the show know, it's a story about an orphan who gets adopted by the richest man in New York. The music and the dancing are sensational, and I once watched it three times in one day. I know I'm not an orphan like Annie, but I can relate to her sense of abandonment. Not that either of my parents physically abandoned me, but I do believe I experienced some emotional abandonment. It took a lot of soul searching and talks with Matty for me to fully understand that concept, but it does help explain why I hate being alone.

Celebrating Christmas again with my parents reminded me of all the good times we had together at this time of year in the past: finding the perfect tree to cut down, stringing Christmas tree lights, midnight Mass at the Polish church, and having dinner at my aunt's house on Christmas day with all of our relatives. My childhood wasn't all bad. We did have good times, especially around the holidays. My parents were here together at my house because they wanted to relive those good times. This was not a day to be sad about the past. I could never be the person I once was again. I didn't want to be. I liked being Jessica, even with all of the hardships I had to endure. Matty was right; I needed to start thinking about the present. There was no way to change what happened in the past and I needed to let go of my sorrows while there was still some time for the future.

Something had changed though. My mother didn't seem like such a mean person anymore. She looked frail, and she had a hard time walking upstairs due to osteoarthritis of her knees. Those cold black eyes that I remember chasing me as a kid were no longer there. I didn't need to be angry with her any longer.

I opened my first present—a beautiful set of earrings and a pendant. The next gift was a lotion and body cream set nestled in a lovely pastel green basket with a purple ribbon. The scent was lavender. Then I unwrapped a box of cards with a magnetic snap and a blue-jeweled flower on the front. Each of the cards had pictures of butterfly's, hummingbirds, and flowers on them. There were some other gifts as well: some salted nuts, a Christmas tree ornament of a dancing ballerina, and some scented soap packaged in a pretty box.

Abby got her share of toys, too, including a little ball that was voice-activated; it talked to her when she nudged it. It was so funny watching her chase that ball around the living room. It was made of a material she couldn't chew through, and it housed an electronic gizmo that repeated about a half dozen phrases like "Oh no" and "Bada bing, bada boom."

At one point, my dad napped in his armchair while my mom and I sat on the couch together. The TV was on, but we weren't paying much attention to it. I knew I had to say something. It wasn't right to just sit there without talking, but I didn't know quite what to say to her.

It would be rude not to say anything, and I loved the gifts she and my dad had given me. This was not the same person who had chased me around the house with a leather strap. That person lived a long time ago, and just as I had gone through a metamorphosis, so had she. No, the woman sitting next to me wanted me to love her. She was looking for my acceptance, and she was reaching out to me for another chance. I didn't need to forgive her with words; I needed to give her some gesture of kindness and to let her know I appreciated what she had done for me.

I turned toward her and said, "You know, I miss not having a childhood as a little girl."

She smiled. "But you did get to play the part of a little a girl once. Remember? You were about twelve years old, I think, and the Parks and Recreation Department put on an outdoor stage show. You volunteered to play the role of a girl, and I helped you with your costume. We made a dress from a white sheet and put a kerchief on your head; I let you borrow one of my red lipsticks. I even helped you apply it to your lips."

I took a moment to recall that day. I had forgotten all about it, but that was probably the first time I had a chance to wear girl's clothes, and I remember how happy it made me feel. It was also one of the few times I remember doing something exclusive with my mother and seeing her smile. It's funny she remembered that.

When it came time for the show, I went out on the stage by myself and improvised my role. It was my first attempt at expressing my gender identity in public with an audience. People heckled me and a friend of my dad asked me if I wanted to go out on a date with him, but that was OK. It was all supposed to be in fun, part of the show, but I had a hard time not letting on that I wished I could dress like that all the time.

How lucky I was compared to many of the transgendered people I know. My parents had come to accept me for who I was, and they realized that it didn't matter what sex I preferred to be. They were going to love me no matter what. Sometimes I get so lost in the ills of my childhood that I forget that.

CONQUERING MY INHIBITIONS

Blackbird singing in the dead of night
take these broken wings and learn to fly
All your life
you were only waiting for this moment to arise.
—The Beatles

We all knew our places. I was stage left, holding my arms in a diagonal as I waited for the tempo of the music to change. Dance had become such a big part of my life. Four nights out of the week and sometimes on Saturday morning, I took classes in jazz, tap, ballet, contemporary, and hip-hop. Not that I was any good at it, as I was likely the slowest learner and most awkward student in the school, but there was something about dance that intoxicated me and I was determined to persevere.

Dance is an art, an expression of our individual sense of beauty. It has geometric form and must look free flowing. To become entranced in the

182

dance, breathe in its essence, and attempt to let go of all my inhibitions often put me in a quandary. I worried that I might accidentally project some part of me that's male. Dear me, why on earth should that matter?

In order to be a good dancer, you need to know how to count dance steps. I, who had survived calculus and organic chemistry in college and the rigors of medical school, could not for the life of me memorize eight simple steps in a sequence sometimes. What part of my brain did I need to use to make this happen?

Samantha was an excellent dancer and teacher. She was vibrant, alive. I envied the way she moved across the floor with such fluidity that her dance appeared effortless. Whenever I tried to go to a place in my head where I could hear the music in the same way she did, I could never quite find it.

I knew that I would never be anything more than a level one dancer, but that was OK. I was happy to be accepted by the other girls and to share in the experience with them.

Regardless of my ineptitude, I wondered how differently my life might be had I not discovered dance. It had become such a big part of my existence. I was fascinated by it, but what made it so special? I never thought of dance when I was younger.

I can no longer recall the first time I entered the dance studio or how I found the school. Maybe it was an ad I saw in the newspaper, or maybe I searched the Yellow Pages. I'm not sure any more. Most of the girls were teenagers, but there was a group of adults who came to class regularly, too. The first class I ever took was jazz, but soon afterward I started taking tap and ballet. It was such a joy to be there.

I remember going to buy ballet shoes for the first time and finding that the straps weren't attached. I thought they were defective. I asked the saleslady if she'd take them back and give me a new pair.

She responded, "No, dear, you have to sew them on yourself."

"Really?" I was dumbfounded. "You have to sew them on yourself? Do all ballet slippers come like that?"

She must have thought me incredibly naive as it took her a moment to formulate a reply.

"It's because everyone's foot is a little different. Would you like me to show you how to do it?"

I nodded in the affirmative, looking at her somewhat timidly.

"You should put the shoe on first…yes, that's right. Now one side of the ribbon goes here," she said, pointing to my mid-foot. "You now stretch it across and attach it on the other side. It's important that you don't sew along here." She pointed to where the purse string ran. "That's it. You do the other strap the same way and you're done."

I know it sounds silly, but I often feel special learning something that only women are generally interested in. I love being a girl. I can't help but think how fortunate I am. In a world where sex is so binary, and people expect you to be either male or female with no in between, it is gratifying to know that I pass well enough that I can do most anything I want to.

Not once in any of my classes did anyone question my gender. I'm sure some people knew my history, but no one asked me about it. I was glad, because I didn't want the focus to be on me. I'm sure if I was still a guy and taking ballet, people would have wondered if I were gay. I suppose I shouldn't care about such things as that anymore, but I grew up in time when people ostracized you for being gay, lesbian, or transgendered. During my youth, the people in my small town weren't even aware of the concept of gender diversity. People like that were just freaks and didn't deserve to live.

My fears of dancing were tempered by the fact that Samantha was a professional. She was not one to easily get upset with any of her students, especially if she felt you were trying. She had the patience of a saint. If she did criticize you, it was because she felt you had the ability to be better and you weren't performing to your potential.

"OK, girls, I want you all to move to center stage. Tonight we are going to try something different," she exclaimed as she half-winked with a little twinkle in her eye.

Oh no. We all knew what that meant. We were going to have to do something designed to help us lessen our inhibitions. I took contemporary dance class with her in part because I knew this was part of her routine.

"I want you all to lie on the floor. We're going to do something I like to call mac and cheese."

She dimmed the lights and turned the music on from her iPod. A soft African drum played in the background as we spread out across the dance floor. Once we were all comfortable and in position, she began guiding us through the dance.

"Now I want you to just move your fingers."

"Now your toes."

"Next your head."

"Now your pelvis."

"Now move your arms...and next move your legs."

By this point we were all slithering to and fro along the dance floor.

"OK, now glide over to the person next you."

"Yikes! Here it comes. She's going to ask us to do something that could be embarrassing," I said to myself.

"Now I just want you to melt into the person you're with. Imagine them as the most comfortable couch you've ever laid on."

Oh my God! I closed my eyes and tried to relax. I knew my partner was feeling the same anxiety I was. "It's OK, Jessica, just let yourself go," I told myself. Part of me was scared to death, and the other part was feeling overwhelming joy for accepting the challenge.

How had I gotten to this point? What a journey I had been on. Whenever I took the time to try to analyze my situation, I found it difficult to fathom how I ever got from point A to point B.

Letting go of inhibitions has been a big part of my existence. In the beginning, when I was a preteen, what started as simple cross-dressing gradually became more encompassing. As time went on, I wanted more. I wanted a woman's body, and I wanted to know what it felt like to be a woman. Although I have a good imagination, I wanted the experience to be real.

Painting my toenails, wearing women's undergarments, shaving my legs, getting tattooed with fairies and butterflies, taking hormones, pursuing permanent hair removal with laser and electrolysis, and eventually having gender reassignment surgery were all progressively more daring things that I did as I got older to satisfy my sexual being. It was as if I was always pushing the envelope. Opening up to Dr. Gransby and finding Dr. Braunwald were landmark events in my life, and what happened to me after meeting them was truly transforming.

In some ways, surgery was not an end result for me but rather a new beginning. I've always felt heterosexual, and after surgery I started dating men because it didn't seem right to have a same-sex partner anymore. The first time I kissed a man felt very strange, but I kept telling myself, "It's OK, Jessica. You're a girl now, and this is acceptable behavior." Needless to say, I had a similar dialogue with myself the first time I stood at a ballet bar. If only I could have found my passion forty years earlier.

I don't believe I became a woman simply to have a male sexual partner. I could have done that without surgery. Female gender identity and gender role were just as important to me.

My dating experiences likely parallel those of a biological woman. It felt awkward at first, and I wasn't sure how to play my part. I often felt insecure and hopelessly afraid that my life would end before I'd find an endearing mate, but then I met Calvin and everything changed. He knew of my background but wasn't afraid of intimacy with me. He helped me solve the mystery that had been elusive to my female self. What I experienced with him was passion. I liked his scent. In his arms, I explored every muscle of his body and when he kissed me, I closed my eyes and found ways to communicate with him without words. After a while, I knew his rhythm, his touch, the way he tasted, the strength of his back, and the ruggedness of his face. I knew when he needed a break from me, and I knew when he was thinking of me. I felt protected when I was with him. With his help, I learned how to experience love as a woman, and I unraveled its mystery. The hermaphroditic earthworm was one of the few other creatures on earth that could relate to my experience. How crazy is that?

As a man, I had experienced these same feelings with Madge many years ago. I now knew something that was rare and that very few people in this world would ever be privileged to know. I had been loved both as a man and a woman. I had eaten from the apple in Eden.

The desires of men and women aren't really that different. I believe sexual eroticism is in part a learned response. Visual imagery of a pleasurable moment contributes to our desire to repeat the event. Since I knew from my previous life what sexual pleasure felt like, it was just a matter of time and experience before I could reproduce that feeling again, although the connections in my brain had to be relearned in a sense.

As I lay propped across my dance partner's midsection, I thought about all of the good things that had happened in my life. The African drum was still playing in the background, and I was feeling quite pleased with myself. Like the butterfly inked to my chest, I was free now to be whoever I wanted to be.

THE FINAL TRUTH

A soft violin and maybe an oboe were playing in the background, a little night music, as I liked to call it. Most evenings, when I go to bed now, I like to listen to classical or ballet music. It's soothing and helps me fall asleep. I always have so much on my mind. I can obsess about things and rethink a situation a thousand times over. The music helps me focus on something that has a steady progression. It holds my attention and doesn't let me get bogged down on any one particular thought.

Writing this story has been more than just a means of self-expression. It's had a healing effect, too. In many ways it's like painting. You start by putting some words and sentences down on paper, hoping they will help express an idea or a set of emotions to the reader. Just as in painting, you rework the canvas—changing a word here and another one there, expanding on an idea by building new paragraphs, or simply stepping away for a while and getting a fresh point of view. It's my hope that my writing gives people a better sense of what it's like to live with gender dysphoria.

There are times when I question my existence, when nothing appears real, and everything around me seems imagined. It's like I'm in a dream. Who could have possibly written this script for me? It's too fantastic to imagine that I could have created it myself, yet here I am playing the leading role. It's an incredible story, but to play my part borders on insanity.

In becoming Jessica, I couldn't escape the disappointments of my earlier life. I had to accept that life wasn't always fair and the nurturing I never had as a child was not something I could fabricate using other people as the adult. Trying to force Dr. Braunwald to take on that role wasn't the answer. What we shared between us was "transference," a psychoanalytic phenomenon whereby feelings I had for my biological mother were redirected to her. Transference is a powerful force. Even though I had medical knowledge of the concept, a part of me wanted to deny its existence.

To her I was probably just another difficult patient, but in my mind she contributed to my creation, and I longed for her forgiveness. When she cut off communication with me, I grieved her loss. She proclaimed to be an expert in transgender behavioral health, but she couldn't understand me. I was the monster in the book *Frankenstein*. My obsession with her came from never having a chance to get to know her.

Finding a way to get past my sorrow has not been easy. I've traveled to the ends of the earth, or so it seems sometimes, looking for peace. Although I have no desire to be a man again, changing my sex and my gender has not solved all of my problems. Those basic needs—the desire to be loved, financial security, and having good health—are unchanged. Although I love waking up in the morning to more choices than simply brown or black shoes, I often still feel like something is missing. All my achievements, such as surviving medical school, transforming myself into someone else, and even opening my own business, never seem enough, but who am I trying to please? Is it an inner need for maternal love?

I have come to the realization that my mother does love me. She's just had her own lessons to learn. Knowing now that she is trying to make things better between us helps me find the peace I've been searching for.

She had a tragic childhood, and only recently did she share the details with me and allow me to ask questions. I will never know the sadness she must've felt when her younger brother drowned at the age of four. How horrifying it must have been for her when they found his body. Her parents separated soon after, and according to my mom, my grandfather could never forgive my grandmother for letting the child play near the water unattended. Shortly afterward, he went off to fight in World War II. While he was away, my grandmother lost her sight and was diagnosed with a brain tumor. When he returned from the war, he didn't believe at first that his wife was blind or that she had a brain tumor and thought maybe she was pretending. After her death, my grandfather remarried, and my mother and her two surviving brothers lived again with him briefly. From here the details are a little sketchy, but my mom tells me she and her brothers didn't get along very well with their stepmother. Their father, not wanting to take care of them any longer, asked relatives to take them. Eventually her two brothers were adopted, but my mom was sixteen by then and too old for adoption. Instead, she was placed in foster homes until she was old enough to fend for herself.

I can no longer hold my mother accountable for the traumas I experienced in my childhood now that I can see, in a broader context, what she had to endure.

As for Dr. Braunwald, I don't know if she will ever be able to see me within my own dimension. It's not right for me to blur professional boundaries, yet I want so much for her to know how it feels to be me. I struggle with being alone, with feelings of emptiness, and a sense of abandonment. Could it be that what I really want is to be able to communicate those feelings to my biological mother? Maybe I already have.

I draw strength from my family, my friends, and my patients. I joined a Unitarian church a few years ago, after learning about it from Dr. Braunwald, and became part of a covenant group that meets once a month on a Sunday evening. There are eight of us, all from different backgrounds. After a short check-in, we like to philosophize about all aspects of life and religion. It's such a joy to be with them. Two are teachers, one worked for a state senator, one is a law librarian, one is a therapist, one grew up in South Africa, and one is a nurse. They are my safe haven, a place where I can go and be accepted, a place where I am looked up to for my accomplishments.

I have always been amazed by the cohesiveness of the group. It's rare for one of us not to show up. We are intellectuals, and our discussions, like our lives, are always varied and free-spirited. We start each meeting by lighting a candle, and whoever volunteered the month before to be the leader picks the topic and starts us off by reading a passage from a book, the lyrics to a song, or a poem. One night, when it was my turn, I chose to talk about atonement.

It was a topic I knew all too well. The definition of atonement is sometimes interpreted as a need for forgiveness in conjunction with some form of reparation for a wrongdoing. Decisions I made adversely affected other people. Was it wrong for me to want to be who I am? If indeed, my brain was sexed female and I was simply born in the wrong body, did I need to hold myself accountable for other people's suffering? Those are hard questions for me to answer. I struggle with them all of the time.

Life is about making difficult decisions. Consider the shell-shocked Vietnam vet who recalls, in the heat of battle, calling in artillery to save his friends only to find that women and children in a small village are killed because of his decision. He did what he felt was necessary at the time, but he still has to live with the consequences of his actions. Did he make the right decision? If he did nothing, many of his friends would have died. In my opinion, he did what he had to do; there was no choice for him. However, if he's like most of us with a conscience, he'll probably struggle to forgive himself. It's human nature.

I have to live with the consequences of my actions, too. What if I'd waited? What if I'd just continued to live as the person I was without changing? There were powerful forces working inside me that I will never fully understand. Had I not transitioned, I believe I would have died. Maybe not in the physical sense, but I would have been like a hollow reed, existing but having no life inside of me.

Since it's impossible to reclaim my childhood, I need to focus now on the future. Certainly writing this book has been an accomplishment for me, but where do I want my life to go from here? Maybe I've said all I need to say for now. Maybe it's time to start learning how to cook better, go skiing with Calvin, take some ballet classes with Matty, spend more time with my kids, read more, or take piano lessons. In short, get on with my life. I can't continue to let the sadness of my past eat away at me.

My business is growing, I have moved from a mobile home into a condo, and I have good friends. I have reconciled with my children, and my brother is talking to me again. I am continuing to dance as much as time and a bad knee allow, and life is generally kind to me.

As time goes on, I hope Calvin and I will continue to explore our relationship, I hope Dr. Gransby will continue to stay in touch with me by e-mail and occasional visits together at her office, and I hope Meredith and Matty will continue to watch over me and keep me safe.

Life is truly a journey. Maybe, before we're born, we're all required to draw lots from a hat to see what our next life will be. Wouldn't that be a hoot? It's strange how my mind works sometimes.

AFTERWORD

So that's my story. Everyone I know who's been through a gender change has their own story to tell, but I'm sure if you ask them, few will say they had a choice. It's all about self-preservation.

I'm a survivor. Not everyone who takes this journey is so lucky. I was driven, and that was both a curse and a saving grace for me. Having some financial assets didn't hurt either. One of the hardest things for me to do during my transition was to hold back the excitement I felt inside. Maybe you can remember when you were a kid and you got a new bicycle, a train set, or that Suzy-Q oven you'd been asking for all year. Do you remember how you wanted to tell everyone in the world about it? If you started boasting too much though, it had a negative effect, and you found people didn't want to listen to you anymore. Transition is a lot like that. You have to learn to hold back.

Giving too much information all at once is like a circuit overload, and nothing you say gets through. The struggle for me was always trying to contain my enthusiasm when transition was all I could think about. Speaking to a trained therapist or going to a support group can help. There you'll find a safe outlet for discussions about sex and gender. Ultimately, you'll have to be true to yourself, and to that end, it's likely someone will be hurt by your actions.

When people ask me for advice about transitioning, I often tell them to focus on other things when they're out with family or friends. Talk about the movies playing at the theater, the foods you like to eat, whether rain is expected later in the week, or current events. Show people that you can still be "normal."

Did I follow those rules? No, at least not early on, and it cost me friends, a brother who wouldn't speak to me for over four years, and a marriage.

I believe everything happens to us for a reason, and we are all affected by the people around us. We are all a part of the interconnected web of life.

What then is my charge? I guess the answer to that question doesn't lie in me but in those people who I've developed relationships with and in those whose hearts I've touched.

Who will judge my merits? Have I helped anyone see the world differently? Have I given hope to someone when they've felt lost? Have I treated others fairly?

Recently, I learned that my friend John, who I spoke of earlier in this story, passed away. I regret never having the chance to tell him how much he meant to me. He was once my best friend, and now I'll never be able to speak to him again. I always thought that someday we'd have a chance to reconcile. Now that can never happen. I reach out to him in my thoughts and hope the afterlife affords him a better opinion of me than I have of myself sometimes.

If through my actions, I've hurt anyone intentionally or unintentionally, may I be forgiven?

Learning to find the good in people is an art and, at least for me, it takes practice, but it's very rewarding. I have had an interesting life. As a medical doctor, I have seen many forms of human suffering, but I have also seen acts of kindness, courage, compassion, and the desire for people to want to help each other.

It is my hope that future generations will be more tolerant of each other. I believe we all have our own individual lessons to learn. Wouldn't it be grand if the afterlife afforded us each the opportunity to share our experiences intimately with one another? Time is relative. Maybe each of us lives within the other. Maybe only in death will we all know the truth about each other.

CPSIA information can be obtained
at www.ICGtesting.com
Printed in the USA
LVOW04s1610260116

472355LV00019B/1009/P